twist & twine

18 Ideas for Rag Rugs and Home Décor

Bobbie Irwin

kp

KRAUSE PUBLICATIONS
CINCINNATI, OHIO

mycraftivity.com
connect. create. explore.

media

Published by Krause Publications, an imprint of F+W Media, Inc., 4700 East Galbraith Road, Cincinnati, Ohio, 45236. (800) 289-0963. First Edition.

13 12 11 10 09   5 4 3 2 1

DISTRIBUTED IN CANADA BY FRASER DIRECT
100 Armstrong Avenue
Georgetown, ON, Canada L7G 5S4
Tel: (905) 877-4411

**DISTRIBUTED IN THE U.K. AND
EUROPE BY DAVID & CHARLES**
Brunel House, Newton Abbot, Devon, TQ12 4PU, England
Tel: (+44) 1626 323200, Fax: (+44) 1626 323319
Email: postmaster@davidandcharles.co.uk

DISTRIBUTED IN AUSTRALIA BY CAPRICORN LINK
P.O. Box 704, S. Windsor NSW, 2756 Australia
Tel: (02) 4577-3555

Library of Congress Cataloging-in-Publication Data
Irwin, Bobbie.
  Twist and twine: 18 ideas for rag rugs and home décor /
  Bobbie Irwin.-- 1st ed.
      p. cm.
  Includes bibliographical references and index.
  ISBN-13: 978-0-89689-736-6
  1. Rag rugs. 2. Hand weaving. I. Title.
  TT850.I794 2009
  746.7'4--dc22   2009023954

Edited by Nancy Breen
Designed by Rachael Smith
Photography by Reed Irwin and Al Parrish
Production coordinated by Matt Wagner
Styling by Jan Nickum

Metric Conversion Chart

To convert	to	multiply by
Inches	Centimeters	2.54
Centimeters	Inches	0.4
Feet	Centimeters	30.5
Centimeters	Feet	0.03
Yards	Meters	0.9
Meters	Yards	1.1

Lillie Sherwood

Nate Jones

dedication

In memory of Lillie Sherwood (1900–1993) and Nathan Jones (1915–2001).

acknowledgments

To Lillie Sherwood, my mentor, friend and surrogate grandmother, I owe so much. She taught me to twine rugs, and she also taught me much about living. I still feel her guiding presence when I teach a twining class. She would be delighted to see so many people enjoying rag twining today.

Nate Jones not only proved to me I could twine with rags without any tensioning device, but his incredible innovations and creativity inspired many of the projects in this book. It was a privilege to demonstrate rag twining with him at community events.

During my more than twenty years of research, many dozens of people have helped me along the way. I thank them all. Rag rug makers have been an immense source of information and inspiration; museum personnel have welcomed me into their collections and provided marvelous assistance.

I thank my friends at Krause Publications for publishing my first book, *Twined Rag Rugs*, and for encouraging me to write this one.

Special thanks go to my husband, Reed Irwin, for his excellent and patient photography, for which he was on call for many months; for putting up with stray threads and fabric strips throughout the house; and for his helpful suggestions and clever equipment design and construction.

Introduction

I never intended to make rag rugs; but ever since I first saw twined rugs in 1980, I've had a special fascination with them. I now feel I was chosen to specialize in this technique and directed to bring back a rapidly vanishing folk craft. It's gratifying to see a new generation of rug makers all over the world enjoying rag twining and ensuring that the craft will survive.

Lillie Sherwood, my twining teacher, was an expert and innovative rug maker; destiny sent me to the master to learn. In her younger years, she had twined rag saddle girths and sold them through a leather shop. She twined rag upholstery for a daughter's car. She probably twined other items she never told me about—I saw only her beautiful rugs.

Years later I met Nate Jones, whose creativity with this technique might have surpassed even Lillie's. Nate had never seen a twined rag rug before he made his first one.

Nate had learned how to twine baskets with sea grass, and one day he decided he could do something similar with fabric strips. He started with circular rugs and went on to twine rag bedcovers, picture frames, candlesticks—virtually anything he could think of.

Inspiration from Nate and Lillie led to many of the projects in this book. During my research, I also found or heard of other items twined with rags: carrying straps, lawn chairs, mug mats. Wherever there have been creative rag twiners, there have been people making beautiful and functional items—rugs and more!

When you twine, you are practicing the most ancient textile technique, more than twenty-eight thousand years old. I strongly believe that to perpetuate an old craft, it's important to tie it to the past while putting it in a modern context. Twining is a venerable tradition; and with projects like the ones presented here, it's a tradition that continues to evolve.

What is Twining?

Unless you make baskets, chances are you're not very familiar with the term *twining*. While it's still a prominent textile art in some cultures, twining is little known in the more developed nations.

You may be familiar with twined rugs by a different name. They've been called many descriptive (and misleading) names—braid-woven, cross-woven, paring-woven, woven, frame-braided, Indian tie rugs and herringbone—but rarely by the name which fits them best. Many people who made these rugs had no name for them.

Twining is the oldest textile technique. Archeological evidence from clay impressions suggests twining was relatively sophisticated twenty-eight thousand years ago in what is now eastern Europe. It was probably used to make mats—the precursors of rag rugs. Because textiles are perishable, none that are older than ten thousand years remain, and those that do remain are invariably twined. Twining is much older than weaving.

Twining developed independently in cultures all over the world as a natural way of assembling flexible materials. It survives primarily in basketry and is still an important textile technique in Africa, Asia and other parts of the world.

Twined rag rugs are a much more recent development. They date back to about 1850 when commercial fabric became widely available and affordable. Twining was one of a proliferation of rag rug techniques at that time. Like twining, twined rag rugs developed in different cultures and geographic areas, ranging from the Pacific Northwest of North America to northern Europe. The traditions of European immigrants probably influenced most American twined rag rugs, although most Americans who made these rugs learned the technique from neighbors and friends, not from their own ancestors.

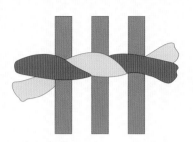

Weft Twining
The brown strands are the warps and the rust and blue strands are wefts.

Wherever people have had access to fabric, they have combined it with other materials in their twining, for both decorative and practical purposes.

Twining Defined

Some people assume a twined rug is made with twine, a twisted cord. The words *twined* and *twine* have the same source, and twining does involve twisting. In all the projects presented here, two flexible stands (called *wefts*) twist around each other to enclose perpendicular strands, called *warps*. This is called *weft twining*. The set of warps, collectively called *the warp*, forms the framework for the textile. Warps are parallel in rectangular projects and radiate from a central point in circular projects.

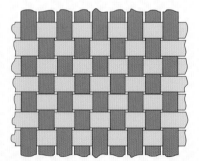

Plain Weave

Twill Weave (above left) and a Twill-Like Pattern in Weft Twining (above right)

Is Twining the Same as Weaving?

Like twining, *weaving* has warps and wefts, and some consider twining to be a form of weaving. In most weaving, a single weft travels back and forth, going over and under warps at regular intervals. Sometimes there is more than one weft, but they either follow the same path or alternate in successive rows.

Weft twining requires at least two wefts that travel in the same direction at the same time, crossing between the warps so that one is on top and one underneath a warp. The use of at least two wefts and the twisting to enclose warps make twining distinct from normal weaving.

Other Fabric Types

A little knowledge of weaving is helpful to understand fabric descriptions in this book.

Plain weave is the simplest and closest interlacement. A single weft passes over one warp and under the next.

In *twill weave*, a weft passes over or under more than one warp at a time for at least part of a row. On the next row, the pattern shifts a bit, resulting in a diagonal pattern that's typical of twill weaves. There are many other types of woven fabrics (made by weaving).

Not all fabrics are woven. For many projects in this book, I've used knit fabrics, created by *knitting*. Knitting is a method of looping that has no warps or wefts.

Twining can resemble some other textile structures. Some forms of twining create diagonal patterns similar to twill. Twining can resemble *braiding* but is not related. Braiding requires three or more strands that work in the same direction while alternately crossing each other. There is no warp, and most braiding forms a narrow strip or cord.

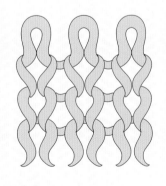

Knitting
Loops without warps or wefts.

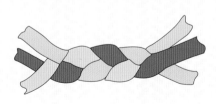

Braiding
Requires three or more strands, but no warps.

Basic Twining Terminology

Throughout this book, I'll repeat certain terms. Here are the ones I use most often.

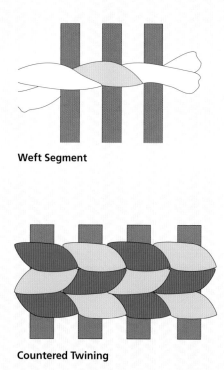

Weft Segment

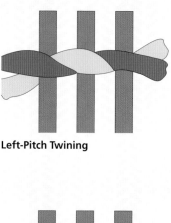

Left-Pitch Twining

Countered Twining

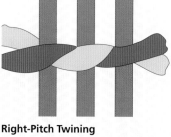

Right-Pitch Twining

Weft Segment
A *weft segment* is the portion of weft that appears on the surface; it's created every time a twined weft crosses over one or more warps. In the illustration above, the weft segment is blue.

Left-Pitch and Right-Pitch Twining
Twisting makes weft segments slant. A *left-pitch* weft segment (above, top) slants up to the left; a *right-pitch* weft segment (above, bottom) slants up to the right. You can see the same slant in twisted twine, string and yarn, although in those examples the slant usually is not referred to as *pitch*.

Normally all segments in a single row should have the same pitch.

Countered Twining
In countered twining, the pitch changes from one row to the next. Most of the rectangular projects in this book use countered twining because it keeps the corners from curling. The twist direction in one row counteracts the opposite twist in the next row.

I also refer to this technique as *regular twining* to distinguish it from *same-pitch twining* (see page 9).

Same-Pitch Twining
In *same-pitch twining*, successive rows have the same pitch.

In a basket or curved rug, the angle of the warps changes frequently; consequently, same-pitch twining does not cause curling. However, when warps are parallel, the finished textile curls. For this reason, I rarely use same-pitch twining in a rectangular rug, or at least I confine it to narrow pattern bands since curled corners present a safety hazard.In rectangular twining, depending on how you turn at the sides, two types of patterns develop when the wefts are different

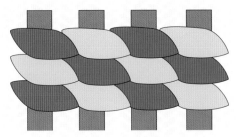

Same-Pitch Twining with Left Pitch

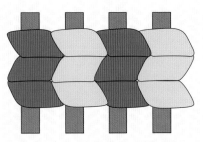

Vertical Columns in Countered Twining
Note the chevron pattern.

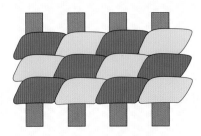

Same-Pitch Twining with Right Pitch

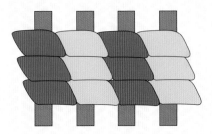

Vertical Columns in Same-Pitch Twining
Note the sawtooth edges.

colors. You can achieve a checkerboard effect, where colors alternate both horizontally and vertically, or vertical columns, where colors line up. Both of these designs are incorporated in the basic sampler (page 38).

In same-pitch twining, the same patterns develop, but the consistent pitch gives a somewhat different effect.

Additional Terms

A *selvedge* is a finished edge of a textile that forms automatically (or naturally) and requires no special treatment to keep it from raveling. I use the term primarily to refer to the finished sides of a fabric or of the rectangular textile I twine. *Selvedge warp* means the warp at the side of a woven or twined textile. However, one of the beauties of rectangular twined textiles is that they also can have selvedges at the top

and bottom. Even irregular twined pieces may have finished edges that can be considered selvedges.

As applied to rugs, *rag* means fabric, whether recycled or new. A *rag rug* is one made primarily from fabric, and twining is one of dozens of ways of making rag rugs. A *twined rag rug* has fabric wefts and often fabric warps as well.

A *loom* is a device used to hold warps under tension. A frame is the simplest type of loom. A *Salish loom* is a simple upright loom.

A *standard or conventional loom* is a floor or table loom for working horizontally, usually for weaving. It has foot treadles or levers to raise and lower warp threads. Many weaving looms have a means to adjust tension, to store extra warp and finished cloth and to keep the working area easily within reach.

Chapter One

Equipment and Tools

One of the beauties of twining is its appeal for people of all incomes and experience levels. Chances are, you already have much of the equipment you'll need around your house, and other items you might need are readily available at low cost. It's even possible to twine wonderful rugs and other projects with little more than scissors, a needle, scrap fabric—and your imagination!

A few companies now sell frames specifically designed for making twined rag rugs. While they incorporate some convenient features, you can make a perfectly good rug on a very simple frame you make yourself. This is one reason twined rag rugs have been especially popular during periods of economic hardship: Anyone who had scrap fabric could afford to make a rug. In the past, twined rag rugs were made most frequently by people who did not have standard looms.

A rug frame needn't take up a lot of space in your home. There are features you can incorporate into a frame that make twining more comfortable and convenient and allow you to make projects of different lengths on the same frame. Selvedge guides—as simple as spaced pegs or straight wires—can help keep the sides of your rugs straight. A built-in easel keeps a frame upright and assists in rotating a frame to work from both ends.

Wherever people have twined rag rugs, they have come up with equipment variations to make the process easier. Just as twining itself developed independently worldwide, so have similar equipment styles, to meet the universal needs of rug makers. This chapter will show you how to build a frame that fits your needs, as well as give you information about other equipment you'll want for additional projects in this book.

Sampler Frame

If you are just learning twining, start with stretcher bars to make a simple frame for the basic twining sampler in Chapter Three (page 38).

Stretcher bars (also called canvas stretchers) are available in many art, hobby and needlework stores. They are sold by length and range in size from about 4" (10cm) up to 8' (2m). (The stated length of a stretcher bar is the outer dimension; the inside length of most brands—the approximate size of the twined article—is about 3½" [9cm] less than the outer dimension.)

Stretcher bars fit together without special tools, and they are inexpensive enough that you can assemble a collection of many sizes to make frames of various dimensions. Buy the bars in pairs.

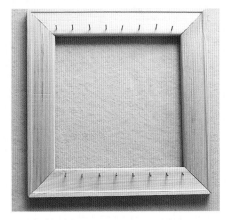

Frame from Stretcher Bars
This small frame is just right for making samplers.

Building the Sampler Frame

For the *Basic Twining Sampler (Hot Pad)* (Chapter Three), use four 11" (28cm) stretcher bars (or another flat, sturdy frame with an inside measurement of 7½" [19cm] square). Most bars have slotted ends that fit together to form a frame with mitered corners. (Since stretchers are made of unfinished wood, humidity can make it tricky to fit them together tightly.) Artists use wooden wedges to secure the corners permanently, but for twining this isn't necessary—it's not crucial that the assembled frame be exactly square. By ignoring the wedges, you can disassemble a frame for storage and use parts of it with other sizes of bars for different projects.

Twining Frames

Most twined rag rugs in the American and European traditions have been made on frames approximately the size of the desired rug. A few have been twined on hoops, such as old wagon wheels or bicycle rims. A frame holds warps under tension and keeps them aligned. Working on a frame is an easy way to learn twining.

A twining frame can be as simple as something nailed together out of scrap lumber, or it can be elaborate enough to adjust for different sizes of projects. All can be made easily and inexpensively with materials from almost any hardware store or lumberyard using simple tools, such as a saw, drill, screwdriver and pliers or wrench. A frame is under little tension as you twine, so standard 1" × 2" (25mm × 51mm) lumber is strong enough.

Across the top and bottom of the frame, nail brads (small ⅞" [22mm] finishing nails) about ⅜"(10mm) from the inside edge of the stretcher bars. Space the brads 1" (25mm) apart, extending about ⅝" (16mm) from the frame's surface. For the traditional 1" (25mm) nail spacing, start ¼" (6mm) from the left edge at the top and ¾" (19mm) from the left edge at the bottom, so the nails are staggered. If the wood is hard, drill small pilot holes first so the nails don't split the wood. Angle the nails slightly toward the top and bottom so the warp won't slip off while you twine.

Even if you are familiar with twining and decide to skip the sampler, you'll find it handy to have this size frame for trying out new fabrics and techniques. It's much easier to sample with a little fabric before you cut the supply for a large project and (maybe) discover that a different strip width would work better.

Stretcher Bars for Larger Frames

Two projects in this book (*Placemats* and *Pillow* in Chapter Six) use longer stretcher bars. The outside dimensions are given; subtract 3½" (9cm) to get the more important inside dimension if you are making your own frames or using nonstandard stretcher bars. Stretcher bars are excellent for large rug frames as well as smaller projects, and they disassemble for storage.

Nail spacing of 1" (25mm) is traditional and gives a spacing of two warps per inch, typical for rugs but not for the lighter-weight projects in this book. For the placemats in Chapter Six (page 93), ⅔" (17mm) spacing gives three warps per inch (25mm); ½" (13mm) spacing gives four warps per inch (25mm). Choose the spacing that fits your needs and your twining habits.

Taking the Frame Apart

To disassemble a stretcher bar frame, place it with the point of a corner on a hard surface and push gently. The frame will collapse easily.

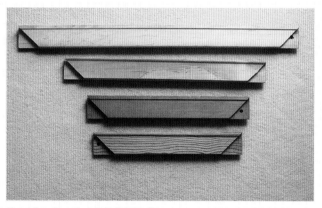

Stretcher Bars in Varied Lengths

Adjustable Pegged Rug Frame

Pegged frames with nails or dowels to hold the warp are the easiest to use because they keep warps in order. Almost all American twined rugs have been made on these frames; however, I do not prefer them for rugs (see *Frame with Suspended Wires*, page 15).

Although stretcher-bar frames are convenient and require no tools except a hammer to insert nails, they are more expensive than constructing a frame from 1" × 2" (25mm × 51mm) lumber. The adjustable pegged rug frame is economical and adjusts for multiple lengths, from 17" (43cm) to 48" (122cm), and will twine an item up to 36" (91cm) wide. Simply move the crossbars to suit your needs.

You can make the rectangular rugs in this book, as well as some of the smaller projects, on an adjustable pegged frame.

Constructing the Frame

To make the adjustable pegged rug frame, you'll need a saw, a pencil, a drill or drill press with ¼" (6mm) bit, a hammer, clamps, wood glue and sandpaper. See the table on page 14 for a listing of wood and hardware requirements.

Cut the Wood

Choose straight, quality lumber. Mark and cut both pieces of wood straight across at 51" (130cm), 90" (229cm) and 93" (236cm) from one end. You should have four 3" (8cm) blocks, two 39" (99cm) crossbars and two 51" (130cm) frame sides. Sand the crossbars and blocks.

Mark and Drill the Sides

With a pencil, lightly mark a lengthwise center line on all four long pieces, then mark the midpoint of each line. On the 51" (130cm) side pieces, mark 24" (61cm) from the midpoint in each direction. Starting at the 24" (61cm) mark on one end of a side and working toward the midpoint, make six marks at 3" (8cm) intervals. From the other 24" (61cm) mark, make 9 marks at 2" (5cm) intervals. Drill ¼" (6mm) vertical holes, centered, at each mark (including the 24" [61cm] marks) except at the midpoint. Repeat for the second side piece. Sand to smooth the wood and remove the pencil marks.

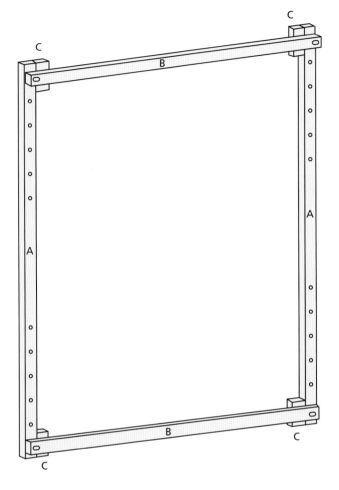

Adjustable Pegged Frame
The nails in the crossbars are not shown. This frame was designed by Reed Irwin; the illustration is based on his original drawing.

Create the Crossbars

On each of the 39" (99cm) sections (crossbars), begin at ¼" (6mm) left of center and measure 18" (46cm) in both directions; mark at 1" (25mm) intervals. Reverse one of the crossbars so the marks are offset by ½" (13mm). Label one crossbar as the top and the other as the bottom; the first mark at the top left should be closer to the edge of the crossbar than at the bottom left.

Drive a nail at each 1" (25mm) mark, with the nail head extending about ⅞" (2cm) from the surface (not

Materials for an Adjustable Pegged Frame

	Quantity	Size	Description	Comments
Wood	2	1" × 2" × 8' (25mm × 5cm × 2m)	pine or fir	2 pieces 51" (130cm), for sides (A)
				2 pieces 39" (99cm) each, for crossbars (B)
				4 pieces 3" (8cm) each, blocks for crossbars (C)
Hardware	4	¼" × 2" (6mm × 5cm)	bolts	
	4	¼" (6mm)	wing nuts	to fit the bolts
	72	4d	bright finishing nails	pegs for crossbars (about 2¼ oz. [64g])

deep enough to go through to the other side). If the wood is hard, drill small pilot holes first to discourage splitting. Angle the nails slightly upward for the top crossbar and downward for the bottom crossbar. The left nail at the top should be ½" (13mm) closer to the side than the left nail at the bottom. Drill a ¼" (6mm) hole ¾" (19mm) from each end of the crossbars on the center lines. Sand off rough edges and pencil marks.

Attach the crossbars to the side ends with bolts and wing nuts (wing nuts on the back), nails facing forward and angled away slightly from the center of the frame. Measure diagonally across the corners (e.g., upper left corner to lower right corner), adjust so they are equal and tighten the wing nuts.

Add the Blocks

Glue and clamp the short blocks to the backs of the crossbars. The blocks should be centered and tight against the inside edges of the sides, extending ¾" (19mm) at the top and bottom of each crossbar.

While the glue is still wet, recheck and adjust the diagonal measurements, repositioning the blocks and clamps, if necessary. Be sure to keep glue off the sides. If you wish, after the glue dries, nail the blocks to the crossbars from the back side for extra strength, using small finishing nails.

The blocks are important to keep the frame square. The 2" (5cm) and 3" (8cm) hole spacings allow 1" (25mm) adjustments in length (except for 18" [46cm] and 47" [119cm] spacings). Another option is to drill the sides at 1" (25mm) intervals. When you're not using the full width of the frame, center the warp on the crossbars.

Selvedge Guides

It's not hard to keep the sides straight when you're twining small pieces, but straight selvedges are more difficult the larger the project. Many twiners have come up with selvedge guides to help keep the edges straight. None is foolproof, but they do help.

The simplest selvedge guides are nails or pegs down the sides of a frame, often positioned about 4" (10cm) apart (not practical on the pegged frame). You can hook rows of twining onto the nails as you work, after you've turned at the edges with the wefts. You can also use cord zigzagged around the frame sides and through the twined edges to hold the sides straight.

The frame on page 15 uses vertical wires. Twine around the wire and the selvedge warp together (treating the wire as part of the warp), and pull out the wire when the project is finished.

Frame with Suspended Wires

When I'm making a rug and want firm twining, I much prefer a frame with suspended wires. This kind of frame lets the materials themselves and the tightness of the twining determine the warp spacing.

You can use stretcher bars with wires instead of nails to make this frame. Music wire (piano wire) works best because it's very stiff at a small diameter and less likely than softer wire to bend as you work. It's available in 1-yard (1m) lengths at hobby shops that cater to builders of model airplanes. You can overlap the wires for wider projects.

Reed's Ultimate Twining Frame
The instructions that follow explain how to build a frame that allows infinite adjustments for rugs up to 36" × 54" (91cm × 137cm)—30" (76cm) wide when selvedge guides are in use—and permits tension adjustments during use.

The frame rotates at its midpoint on its support for twining from both ends of the rug (the traditional way of working). It mounts sideways on the same stand for rugs that are wider than they are long. Optional selvedge guides for the long and shorter edges adjust for different rug sizes and can be removed in order to use the full frame dimension. The suspended wires permit different warp spacings.

While far more elaborate than most traditional frames, it's also much more versatile. My husband designed it to my "impossible" specifications, and I use it for most of my large projects. I call it Reed's Ultimate Twining Frame.

Constructing the Frame
To make Reed's Ultimate Twining Frame, you'll need a pencil, saw, drill or drill press with ¼" (6mm) and ³⁄₁₆" (4.5mm) bits, hammer, screwdriver appropriate for the screws, clamps, wood glue and sandpaper. See the table on page 17 for a listing of wood and hardware requirements.

Assembling the Frame and Supports
With a pencil, mark a lengthwise centerline on the narrow side of the two 60" (152cm) pieces (B) and two 36" (91cm) pieces (C).

On the centerline of each piece, mark the midpoint, then the drill-hole locations at 6" (15cm) intervals in both directions from the midpoint (do not mark the ends). Also mark 2½" (6cm) from the ends of the shorter pieces (C) and 3½" (9cm) from the ends of the longer pieces (B). Drill a ¼" (6mm) diameter hole through each mark, including the midpoints.

Use the four drilled sections to construct a frame 60" × 39" (152cm × 99cm). On a flat surface with wide sides facing up, butt the 36" (91cm) top and base pieces (C) inside the 60" (152cm) side pieces (B). Mark all four for assembly.

Position the metal corner braces and mark drill-hole locations for each, adjusting the braces so no hole overlaps a joint. Drill ³⁄₁₆" (4.5mm) holes and fasten a brace on the front and back sides of the frame at each corner with the #10 × 1¼" (32mm) machine screws and nuts.

For the two support uprights, use the 37" (94cm) sections cut from the 1 × 2s (25mm × 51mm) (D). At one end of each piece, draw a 7" (18cm) line lengthwise down the center of the wide side. Mark and drill ¼" (6mm) holes 1" (25mm) and 7" (18cm) from the end along the centerlines.

At the opposite end of each upright, mark and drill offset hole locations for wood screws to attach the 14" (36cm) support bases (A). Center each base

Homemade Unpegged Frame
Lillie Sherwood used this homemade frame, wrapping the warp around heavy steel rods. When removed, the rods left loops at the ends of the warp, to which she tied yarn or fabric fringe. Wires instead of rods let me make unfringed rugs with selvedges on all four sides.

perpendicular to the upright, wide sides together, to form a T. Mark and drill pilot holes smaller than the screws and attach the bases. If you wish, use wood glue to make the joins more secure.

Attach the supports to the frame at the top of the upright with two 2¾" (7cm) stove bolts on each side, with the top bolts through the middle holes in the frame and the support base pieces (A) toward the inside. To rotate the frame during twining, temporarily loosen the top bolts and remove the lower bolts.

Inserting the Wires

Insert eyebolts through the holes at the top and bottom of the frame, with the eyes inside the frame. The eyebolts support the heavier wires that hold the warp.

The bottom eyebolts need nuts both inside and outside the frame to keep them extended during warping. Wing nuts are an alternative to nuts at the top and bottom outside of the frame. Use as many eyebolts as needed for your project to support the wires just beyond the width of the rug—as many as five when the narrow end is up and nine when the wider end is up. You can overlap wires for wider projects.

Open twelve eyebolts slightly so the wire will slide easily into them. Use unopened eyebolts at the center and sides, with opened bolts between, so you can adjust the warp on the wires. Adjust the nuts or wing nuts to keep wires parallel to the ends of the frame.

For short rugs, use threaded rod and coupling nuts to lengthen the eyebolts as needed.

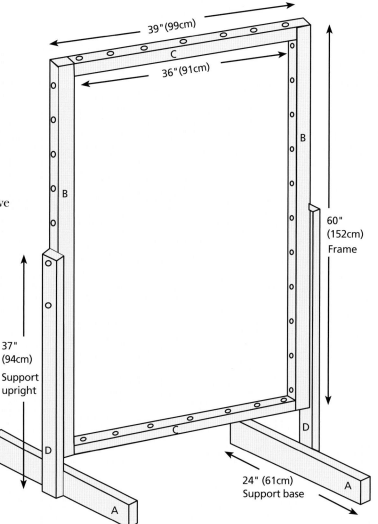

Frame with Suspended Wires

Frame Parts and Dimensions
Letters correspond to the materials in the table on page 17.
Illustration is based on an original drawing by Reed Irwin.

Materials for Reed's Ultimate Twining Frame

	Quantity	Size	Description	Comments & References
Wood (keep all 4 cutoff pieces)	1	2" × 4" × 4' (5cm × 10cm × 122cm)	pine or fir	cut two 24"(61cm) pieces for the support bases (A)
	2	1" × 2" × 8' (25mm × 51mm × 244cm)	pine or fir	cut two 60"(152cm) pieces from each (4 total) for the sides (B) & the long selvedge guides (page 18) use the 2 remaining 36" (91cm) pieces for the top & base (C)
	2	1" × 2" × 8' (25mm × 51mm × 244cm)	pine or fir	cut one 37"(94cm) piece from each (2 total) for support uprights (D) cut one 39" (99cm) piece from each (2 total) for the short selvedge guides (page 18)
Hardware	18	¼" × 5" (6mm × 13cm)	eyebolts	with matching nuts or wing nuts
	18	¼" × 8" (6mm × 20cm)	threaded rod	same thread as eyebolts
	18	¼" (6mm)	rod coupling nuts	same thread as eyebolts
	4	¼" × 2¾" (6mm × 7cm)	stove/machine bolts	same thread as eyebolts
	13	¼" (6mm)	nuts	same thread as eyebolts
	8	#10 × 2½" (6cm)	machine screws	with matching wing nuts
	16	#10 × 1¼" (3cm)	machine screws	with matching nuts
	4	#8 × 1½" (4cm)	wood screws	
	8	2½" (6cm)	flat corner braces	
	36	1" (25mm)	screw eyes	
	4	3mm × 36" (91cm)	music wire	to hold warp
	6	2mm × 36" (91cm)	music wire	for selvedge guides

Constructing Selvedge Guides

To make these selvedge guides, you'll need a pencil, saw, drill or drill press with ¼" (6mm), ³⁄₁₆" (4.5mm) and ³⁄₃₂" (2.3mm) bits, hammer, screwdriver appropriate for the screws you're using, clamps, wood glue and sandpaper. See the table on page 17 for wood and hardware requirements.

Construct two long selvedge guides from 60" (152cm) pieces cut from 1 × 2s (25mm × 51mm). For clamps, cut eight 4" (10cm) and eight 3" (8cm) segments from the leftover pieces of 1 × 2 (25mm × 51mm) .

On the wide side of each long guide, mark a perpendicular line 1½" (4cm) from each end. Glue a 4" (10cm) block inside of and flush with one of the lines, perpendicular to the guide.

After the glue dries, place the guide against the frame with the block tight against the inside edge and parallel to the bottom of the frame. The mark at the other end of the guide should be flush with the inside of the opposite end of the frame (adjust as needed).

Glue another 4" (10cm) block to this end. Drill perpendicular ³⁄₁₆" (4.5mm) holes through each block and guide.

On one end of each selvedge guide, center a 3" (8cm) block on the 4" (10cm) block parallel with the guide, flush with the inner edge and extending beyond the other edge of the longer block. Mark the hole location and drill a ³⁄₁₆" (4.5mm) hole.

Attach the 3" (8cm) block on top of the 4" (10cm) block with a #10 × 2½" (6cm) machine screw and wing nut. Repeat for each end of each guide.

On the wide side of each selvedge guide, mark the center 27" (69cm) from one 4" (10cm) block, then mark every 6" (15cm) in both directions. Drill ³⁄₃₂"-diameter (2.3mm) holes about ½" (13mm) deep at each mark and attach screw eyes, leaving the center of each eye about ³⁄₈" (10mm) above the surface and open to the length of the guide. At each end of a guide, open the last two eyes slightly toward the outside and wide enough to insert the finer selvedge wire.

Construct shorter selvedge guides in the same manner using the 39" (99cm) pieces of 1" × 2" (25mm × 51mm); this is for use when the frame is turned sideways. When using selvedge guides, loosen the wing nuts to move the guides. The distance between the vertical wires should be the desired width of the twining, and the guides must be parallel to the frame sides and the same distance apart at each end.

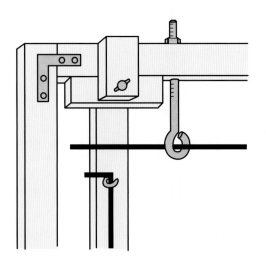

Detail of Frame Corner

This close-up shows one selvedge guide, selvedge wire and suspended wire to hold the warp.

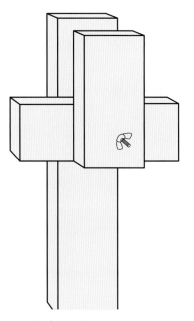

Detail of Selvedge Guide Clamp

Tabletop Salish Loom

Textile historians say twining originally was worked without any loom or frame at all, or on a bar that supported free-hanging warps. Salish people (numerous cultures from the Pacific Northwest of North America) twined bags and other items without tension on the warps. However, once weaving became popular, a tensioning device was needed

After weaving was introduced, Salish people improvised an upright loom for weaving twill blankets on tensioned warps. Their first use of fabric strips in textiles dates to about 1820, when Hudson Bay trade blankets were introduced.

After 1850, when Salish people started twining rectangular rag rugs, they did so on the looms they'd used for weaving blankets. They continued twining rag rugs this way well into the twentieth century. Their simple loom is an ingenious device that essentially folds a project so that half of the warp is on the front side and half is on the back. This lets rug makers weave or twine a long textile on a compact frame.

Traditional Salish looms have elongated notches for the rollers, so tension can be increased or decreased using wedges in the notches. The version presented here provides no tension adjustments. Projects in Chapter Seven (*Twining on a Salish Loom*, pages 102-111) describe how to allow for increasing warp tension.

Two projects in Chapter Seven (*Table Runner*, page 105, and *Photo Album Cover*, page 109) use the same frame, which can make textiles up to 20" × 36" (51cm × 91cm) yet sit comfortably on a table.

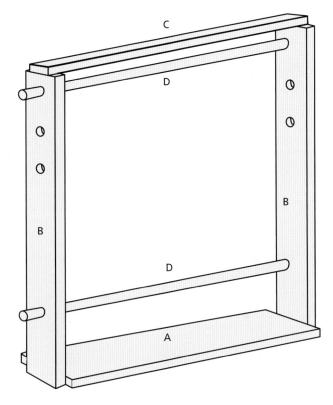

Salish Loom
Letters correspond to materials listed in the table on page 20.

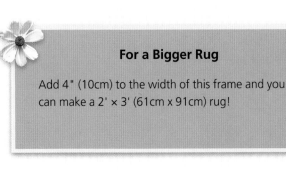

For a Bigger Rug

Add 4" (10cm) to the width of this frame and you can make a 2' × 3' (61cm x 91cm) rug!

Constructing the Loom

To make the Salish loom, you will need a saw, a screwdriver appropriate for the screws you're using, a drill or drill press with ⅛" (3mm), ¼" (6mm) and ¾" (19mm) bits, wood glue, clamps and sandpaper. See the table on this page for wood and hardware requirements.

Cut wood to length and sand smooth. Mark a lengthwise center-line on one wide side of each side piece (B). Along that line on each piece, mark 1⅞" (5cm), 4⅞" (12cm), 7⅞" (20cm) and 19" (48cm) from the top end.

Drill vertical ¾" (19mm) holes at each mark. Sand the holes and the roller dowels (D) so that the dowels will fit closely but still turn within the holes. There should be a little friction.

Place the roller dowels (D) through the top and bottom holes in both sides (B) to assist with aligning the base (A). Glue the bottom of each side to the outside of the base, centered and vertical. Clamp until the glue is dry; remove the dowels. Drill ⅛" (3mm) pilot holes through each side into the base and insert screws.

Center the top brace (C) on top of the sides so the ends of the brace are flush with the outer edge of the sides. Drill a ¼" (6mm) hole vertically through the brace and ½" (13mm) into one side. Insert a ¼" × 1" (6mm × 25mm) dowel into the brace. Check the alignment and drill a hole to attach the other end of the brace on the other side. Glue the small dowels into the holes in the sides, but do not glue the brace to the dowels.

Remove the brace during warping, and replace it for the twining.

Materials for a Tabletop Salish Loom

	Quantity	Size	Description	Comments
Wood	1	1" × 4" × 20" (25mm x 10 cm x 51cm)	pine or fir	base (A)
	2	1" × 3" × 24" (25mm x 8cm x 61cm)	pine or fir	sides (B)
	1	1" × 1" × 21½" (25mm × 25mm × 55cm)	pine or fir	top brace (C)
	2	¾" × 24" (19mm × 61cm)	dowels	rollers (D)
	2	¼" × 1" (6mm x 25mm)	dowels	to fit brace onto sides
Hardware	4	6 × 1½" (4cm)	wood screws	to attach base to sides

Additional Notes on Equipment and Tools

If you already have a standard loom—a floor or table model—you can use it for twining (see page 59). It keeps your working area at a comfortable reach and lets you make a long rug that might not be practical on a frame.

A standard loom has no speed advantage, since twining is entirely hand-manipulated.

In addition to a frame or loom, the following items can be used in twining.

Pin Board

A pin board is a portable and inexpensive way to twine irregular-shaped pieces, such as the curved placemats on pages 93–95. You can also use a pin board for a small rectangular project.

Pin boards are composed of soft, sturdy material that will hold pins firmly but is not so hard that you can't insert pins easily. Buy one at a hobby, craft or needlework shop, or make your own from sound control board (also called sound-deadening panel), ceiling tile or dense foam board. Use it with T-pins or sturdy straight pins.

Creative Forms and Frames

Bowls, pans and boxes provide the framework for some three-dimensional projects—you'll be surprised how many household objects will work! And two of the projects in this book (*Stool Seat* [page 133] and *Chair Seat* [page 136]) remain on the frames on which you work them.

It's not necessary to have any sort of form or frame for some twining, including some rugs and baskets. All of these options are incorporated into the projects in this book.

Cutting Fabric

If you cut a lot of fabric strips with scissors, you'll end up with a sore hand. Pinking shears take more effort to use and leave an undesirable fuzzy edge on the fabric strips. You can buy an expensive rag cutter that clamps to a table, with a vertical blade and crank to turn the blade, but a rotary fabric cutter (like a pizza cutter) and cutting mat with a ruler work very well and cost much less. Both reduce the tendency of woven fabric to ravel better than scissors. Be aware the blades of

rotary cutters as well as scissors dull quickly if you're cutting large amounts of tough synthetic fabrics! If a cutter leaves a line of fabric dust imbedded in the mat, it's time to change blades. You can tear some fabrics, but this maximizes raveling, and the dust (especially from cotton) is a health hazard.

Modifications for Physical Limitations

Almost everyone with some manual dexterity can learn to twine, and rug twining has been an important craft in physical and occupational therapy programs. Its gentle, rhythmic motion is good manual exercise, even for people with severe arthritis.

In one nursing home, a man who had almost no use of his hands for years because of crippling arthritis was able to move his fingers again after he started twining.

You can clamp a frame to a table, vertically for a large frame or horizontally for a small one, for ease of use by people in wheelchairs, or for someone who has use of only one hand. Small portable projects, such as many of those presented in this book, make twining possible for people of all ability levels. Using unsewn joins to connect strips may be easier than hand sewing for those with limited ability to use a needle.

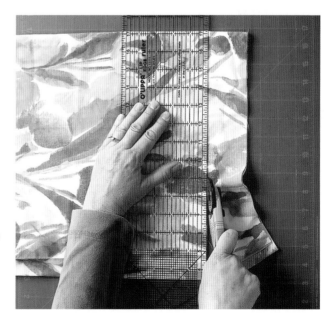

Easy Does It
Cut strips easily with a rotary fabric cutter, mat and wide ruler.

Chapter Two

Fabrics and Twining

The essence of rag twining is fabric in all of its many varieties. Part of the joy of planning a twined project is selecting the fabric. Although the warp is less of a design feature than the wefts, choosing the appropriate material is important to achieve the desired results.

The same fabric can give different effects, depending on its orientation when you cut it. For instance, patterned cloth can take on quite a different appearance in twining. A printed or plaid fabric can produce delightful spots of color as you work, making your finished item appear more complex than it actually is. Sampling will help you develop a feel for the fabrics that work best.

Twining compresses and subdues fabrics, so if you find a fabric that is more flamboyant than you'd choose to wear (but your child or grandchild might wear with pleasure), it will probably make a beautiful rug!

You can combine different types and weights of fabric in the same project as long as you cut them so they will compress to about the same diameter. Knit fabrics are especially easy to work with, since they don't ravel. Woven fabrics are also versatile choices if they are not too loosely constructed.

The tradition of rag work is to use whatever you have available, but don't let the term *rag* fool you. In this context, rag merely refers to fabric. Many wonderful rugs and other projects can be made from new fabrics and remnants. Quilting also has a tradition of using leftover fabric scraps, but these days many quilters have entire stores of exciting new fabrics to choose from. Some quilters take up rag twining because they already have an abundance of fabrics! In fact, quilt fabrics, with their intricate patterns and colors, are wonderful for twined projects.

Warp Fabrics

The best warps (the vertical or lengthwise elements) are strong, flexible and have relatively little stretch and little tendency to ravel. Fabric warps provide a sturdy framework for thick twined textiles such as rugs, and their bulk helps twined rag baskets hold their shape. Some heavy cord is also appropriate for these uses. String warps provide less weight, less bulk and more flexibility where such features are desired.

Fabric Types
Knits
The easiest fabric warps to work with are knits that don't ravel. Most knit fabrics stretch but usually much less cut in one direction than another. Cut warp fabrics in the direction of least stretch, usually parallel to a selvedge. Some knits, such as nylon tricot, are extremely tough and stretch only in one direction. Those containing Lycra® may be too stretchy in any direction. Also avoid bias-cut knits.

Woven
Most woven fabrics stretch less than knits and can be cut in any direction. Choose a tightly woven fabric, preferably plain weave. Although cutting on the bias (diagonal) maximizes stretch, it's usually not a problem in woven fabrics, so you probably can use bias-cut strips if you already have them. While cutting on the bias helps avoid progressive raveling, the cut edges will be quite fuzzy, and you may not want that texture.

Denim fabric is a traditional rug warp. However, it is a twill fabric that ravels easily, and loose threads can interfere with twining. Raveled edges may show through to the surface and detract from the appearance of a rug.

Stitching Continuous Warp
Overlap strip ends at a right angle, then machine-stitch across them diagonally (see page 24).

Color
Warp color is a minor concern, since most warp will be hidden by the wefts. However, the warps do show a bit at the top and bottom of a project, so I usually choose one of the same fabrics or colors I will use for weft at the ends of a project. A dark warp may occasionally show through on the surface when using light wefts, and vice versa.

Considerations When Cleaning
When it comes to cleaning your twining projects, fabric warps can be a problem, especially if the item is densely twined. If a fabric warp becomes wet, it may be difficult to dry and might rot. String warps dry more quickly, and some cord is impervious to moisture.

How Wide?

The width of fabric strips for warp is partly a matter of personal preference. I like a strip that will compress to about the diameter of a pencil, for a warp spacing of two to three warps per inch (25mm). For denim, this might be an inch (25mm) wide; for cotton broadcloth, about 2¼" (6cm) wide. Wool may be even denser than denim and can be cut ¾" (19mm) wide or less, depending on the fabric. I often cut warps a little narrower than I would cut the same fabric for weft.

Preparing Fabric Warps

Never cut your entire warp supply until you have sampled a row or two of twining to see if the width suits your purposes. A small sampler frame is excellent for testing warp and weft widths on a small scale.

Rectangular projects normally start and finish with the same number of warps. Circular and oval projects—rugs and baskets—require the addition of warps as you work. New warps need only be as long as the untwined sections of previous warps, so you can save fabric by calculating the needed length as you work, rather than cutting many long strips ahead of time.

Continuous Warp

For a continuous warp, machine-stitch long strips of fabric together as needed. Overlap the ends at a right angle and sew across diagonally, then trim the excess. This produces a less bulky join than other methods, but sewing straight across is an option. Extra bulk at a seam can usually be hidden by the twining.

Loop Method

Warp loops make preparing a project even quicker. Normally each loop serves as two warps, and all loops should be the same length. If you're using one fabric, cut a rectangle twice as long as the needed warp length plus an inch (25mm) for a half-inch (13mm) seam allowance. The warpwise dimension should be the direction of least stretch.

Fold the rectangle in half, right sides together, and machine-stitch across the top (opposite the fold), then stitch again on top of the first stitching line. The

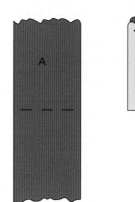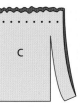

Creating Warp Loops
Fold the fabric (dashed line, A), stitch (dotted line, B), then cut loops (C). Turn the loops right side out. Here, orange is the right side of the fabric.

double stitching helps keep the stitches from coming apart when you cut across the seam. The distance from the fold to the seam should be the desired warp length. Cut loops lengthwise at the desired width.

The loop method gives an even number of warps. If you need an odd number, add a single warp and tuck in the ends later.

Other Warps

String warps are appropriate where light weight and flexibility are needed, or when a finished project may be exposed to frequent moisture. A string warp can be as thick as a fabric warp—heavy cord or clothesline, for example—or much finer. Many of the projects in this book use string warps.

Braided cord or clothesline are options for heavier projects; be aware they tend to be much more expensive than the same length of fabric warp.

Manufacturers make a wide variety of cord to choose from. Worsted-weight four-ply cotton crochet yarn is nice for many projects. It comes in many colors, is inexpensive and is found at many yarn, craft and hobby shops. Several brands are available. I've used it for most of the string warp projects in this book. Consider yarn for warp if it's not too stretchy.

Synthetic cord is a good choice for some items, and natural string such as jute and sisal might work sometimes. Choose according to what's available and what characteristics are important. The chart below shows how the fiber content reacts to different conditions.

If you need to add more warp to get the right length, splice heavy cord together by overlapping ends and sewing through both thicknesses. Join finer string and yarn with knots. The weft will cover the joins, and the extra bulk will not be noticeable. When using synthetic cord, singe cut ends with the flame from a candle or match.

Warp Length and Number

Warp length depends on the project, the equipment and the warping method.

If you know the desired length and warp spacing, you can estimate how much total length you'll need by multiplying individual warp length by warps per inch (25mm). Take the warp width into account when figuring the amount of yardage you'll need (multiply width × length × warps per inch [25mm]).You'll need several inches extra to overlap the ends if you're using a continuous strand, and extra for seam allowance if you're making loops. Bulky fabrics and stout cord take a little more than thinner warps. If I'm using a knit fabric with some stretch, I may use slightly shorter warps than the finished length of a project, because the warp will stretch some as I work.

An Assortment of String Warps

From left to right: polyester braided cord, black nylon string and assorted colors of cotton crochet yarn.

		How Fibers React			
		Resistance to:			
Fiber	**Strength**	**Rot**	**Mildew**	**Sunlight**	**Abrasion**
Cotton	Moderate	Fair	Poor	Good	Fair
Jute	Poor	Good	Good	Good	Poor
Linen	Excellent	Good	Moderate	Good	Excellent
Nylon	Excellent	Excellent	Excellent	Poor	Excellent
Polyester	Excellent	Excellent	Excellent	Excellent	Excellent
Rayon	Poor	Moderate	Poor	Moderate	Poor
Silk	Excellent	Moderate	Good	Poor	Good
Sisal	Poor	Poor	Poor	Excellent	Fair
Wool	Poor	Moderate	Good	Poor	Poor

Some project designs will dictate a specific number of warps; some require an odd number, some even. If you're working from a graph, the number of vertical columns is the number of warps, and that will also be the number of weft segments in a row. For many projects, the number of warps is not critical, and it in part depends on the equipment you're using. When I'm making a rug on a frame with suspended wires, twining tightly, I let the materials themselves determine the spacing, and I use enough warps to achieve the desired width.

How Warps Are Used

The process of aligning warps for twining is called *warping*. There are many warping variations.

On a pegged frame, the most common variation is continuous warping (A, below left), using a single long strand zigzagged back and forth between the top and bottom of the frame. Ending in the diagonally opposite corner from where you started produces an odd number of warps, and ending on the other end of the same frame section where you started makes an even number.

Continuous warping on a frame with suspended wires (B, below center) is most practical if you follow a figure-eight motion between the wires, crossing through the center with each pass. This helps keep the warps in order.

Even easier is warping with loops slipped over pegs or wires (C, below right).

The projects in this book require different types of equipment and warping modifications. Each new version is explained with the project instructions.

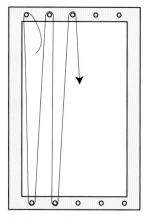

Continuous Warping on a Pegged Frame (A)

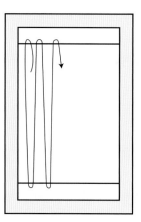

Continuous Warp Around Suspended Wires (B)

Support for the wires is not shown.

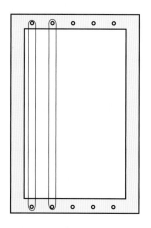

Warp Loops on a Pegged Frame (C)

Weft Fabrics

Can you truly twine with twine? Of course! Basketry materials, yarn and string have been used for thousands of years, much longer than fabric strips. You can use the same techniques and patterns in this book to work with many other materials.

Rag rugs did not become commonplace until about 1850, when commercial fabric became widely available and affordable for most people. Earlier, when most cloth was made by hand, every scrap of fabric was precious, and most fabric was recycled until it was completely worn out.

Twining was one of many rag rug techniques that proliferated after 1850, so the tradition of using rag strips for twining is well established. Fabric strips make twining much quicker than using finer materials such as yarn. The variety of commercial fabrics now available adds to the excitement of twining, enhancing the patterning. Because the wefts are the fabrics that show, choosing weft fabrics is a big part of the fun!

Choosing Weft Fabrics

You have more leeway with weft fabric choices than with warp.

Avoid stiff or bulky fabrics, because flexibility is important. A little stretch is okay, but cut knit fabrics in the direction of least stretch. Extremely stretchy fabrics such as Lycra® are difficult to control. Knits that don't ravel are easiest to work with. Tightly woven fabrics are also practical for many items. Loosely woven fabrics and twills tend to ravel and can be a nuisance to work with; but since I often choose fabrics by color rather than type, I manage to work successfully with most types of woven fabrics.

I have heard that, for rugs at least, it's not wise to combine polyester with cotton or other natural fibers. The polyester is so much tougher that it can cut into softer fabrics. However, you are likely to get many years of use out of a rug before this becomes a serious problem. Otherwise, it's fine to combine fabrics of different weights and types in the same project.

The Effect of Stripe Orientation on Twined Fabric
A striped (left) or plaid fabric will take on a different appearance when twined, depending on how it's cut (below).

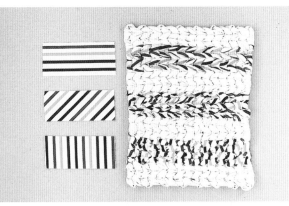

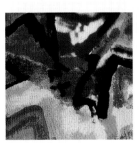

Bold Fabric, Stunning Results
This wild fabric (left) is a wonderful candidate for twining. The resulting twined fabric (above left) is lively and exciting.

Differences in Texture

Knits and woolen fabrics often give a spongy feel to a rug or other project. Some cotton and cotton blends make a firmer texture. Texture depends in part on how tightly you twine, and that depends on your experience, habits and the intended purpose for the piece.

Washing new fabrics, while optional, removes sizing and makes them more flexible and easier to work with. Fabric shrinkage is not a big concern for rugs and other projects that will be cleaned by hand.

Woven fabrics vary tremendously in how easily they ravel. Plain-weave cloth ravels less than twill, and the closer the weave and finer the threads, the less raveling you can expect. Old percale sheets are less prone to raveling than muslin and better than many of today's high thread-count sheets (which often bundle many fine threads into the same row of the weave).

Prints and Color

Twining compresses fabrics and subdues them a bit, so tiny prints may not be very apparent in a twined article. Bright, bold fabrics provide a lot of color excitement. A striped or plaid fabric will take on a different appearance depending on the direction you cut it.

Even after many years of twining, I can't always anticipate how a fabric will look in the twined piece. Quite often it ends up better than I expect! Sampling is always a good idea to avoid disappointment.

An Ancient Form of Recycling

The tradition of twined rag rugs is much more recent than the antiquity of twining itself. However, rag weaving has its own prehistoric precedents.

Across the globe, whenever fabric became available, weavers and twiners have used rag strips to make new textiles. Dozens of ancient textiles recovered from prehistoric ruins in what are now Arizona and Chihuahua, Mexico, were woven with strips of fabric as weft, dating from as early as the thirteenth century. Stashes of fabric strips from at least one archaeological excavation show that this sort of recycling was well planned. Nothing so time-intensive to make as hand-spun, handwoven fabric went to waste.

In more recent centuries, numerous cultures have incorporated commercial cloth in their handmade woven and twined textiles, either as raveled threads twisted into new yarn (such as the Bayeta yarns used by the Navajo) or as strips of cloth for decorative accents. Strands of Hudson Bay blankets appear in Canadian handwoven robes and blankets from the 1820s. A piece of fencing from Africa in the collections of the Smithsonian Institution is twined with vines, fur and cloth wefts, the maker evidently having used whatever was available.

Twined Fence
This section of a fence, collected in Somalia in the early 1900s, is twined with vines, fur and strips of fabric. *Catalog No. 175312, Department of Anthropology, Smithsonian Institution; photo by Bobbie Irwin.*

How Wide Should Wefts Be?

Weft width depends on how tightly you twine, your personal preferences and the purpose for the project. You will develop a feel for gauging weft width as you gain experience, and sampling helps avoid costly errors. Don't cut the entire fabric supply until you're happy with what you're working with. Often ¼" (6mm) difference may make the width just right.

Balance and Compression

While you can combine different types and weights of fabric in the same piece—knits and wovens, sheets and corduroy—you must cut the strips to balance. This means they should all compress to the same size. If you combine a heavy fabric like denim with cotton quilt fabrics, you must cut the lighter-weight material wider.

It's easiest to learn with fabrics of similar weight and type, but don't feel restricted if you find a cloth that's just perfect for the effect you want.

Width According to Fabric Type

For rugs to be twined between two and three warps and rows per inch (25mm), I cut wefts to compress to the diameter of a pencil. In general, this means about 1" (25mm) wide for denim and corduroy, 1½" (4cm) for double knit, 2¼" (6cm) for sheets and lightweight broadcloth and even wider for sheer fabrics.

Wool is a lofty fiber that produces a resilient fabric, and wool fabrics can be cut narrower than other fabrics of comparable weight. For very heavy wools, ½" (13mm) is adequate. Up to 1¼" (3cm) will work for lighter wools. Even with their extra bulk, wool fabrics can twine into surprisingly lightweight textiles.

Fabric width depends on the purpose of the finished item, too. The percale sheeting I cut 2¼" (6cm) wide for a rug works better at 1" (25mm) wide for finer-scale items such as clothing and place-mats. The finished appearance changes with the width.

Use the projects in this book to develop a feel for how you will need to cut your own fabrics.

Segment Size Changes the Appearance

The sampler on the left is twined at two segments and rows per inch (25mm). The album cover on the right is twined from the same fabric, but at four segments and rows per inch (25mm).

Fabric Strips of Different Weights and Widths

These fabric strips compress to the same diameter. Left to right: heavy wool cut at ¾" (19mm) wide, denim at 1" (25mm), double knit at 1½" (4cm) and broadcloth at 2¼" (6cm).

How Long Should Wefts Be?

On a frame-twined piece, pulling wefts through the warps is tedious unless you work with relatively short strips of fabric—usually a maximum of about 2 yards (2m). If your fabric tends to ravel, shorter strips will be more practical.

Because one weft stays on the surface for taaniko twining (see pages 66–67), you can use longer strips for that weft. Twining without tension on the warps also allows longer wefts because you can move the warp into the twist rather than dragging the weft through the warp.

So unless you're using very short scraps of fabric, machine-sewing long strips is not practical for wefts. Instead attach a new strip when you come to the end of an old one or whenever you need to change colors. If you're continuing with the same color, use the same fabric.

Hand Sewing Weft Strips

Hand sewing weft strips is quick, easy and provides a secure join. Neatness isn't important because you can usually hide the joins within the twining.

Overlap strips by about ¾" (19mm) and fold the edges in once or twice (A and B, right). With narrow strips, folding in thirds or in half may be adequate.

Overcast or whipstitch close to the turned-in edge (C, right); it takes only six to eight stitches to secure the edge and tack down the raw edge where strips come together. It's not necessary to sew the entire length of the overlap.

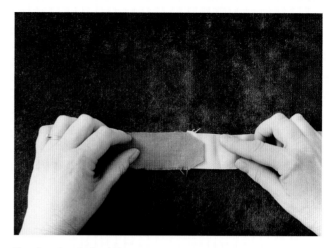

Overlapping Strips (A)
Tapering one or both is an option.

Folding in Raw Edges (B)

Stitching the Join (C)
A different color thread is used in this photo for contrast.

Slit Joins

There are several ways to join strips without sewing, including the use of two slit joins. Sewn joins are more secure for narrow fabric strips, but slit joins are fine for most rug projects.

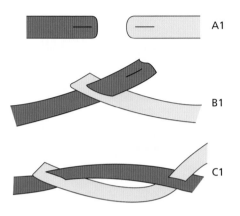

Cut a small slit near the end of each strip (A1, above). Slip the end of the old strip into the slit on the new one (B1, above).

Take the other end of the new strip and insert it through the slit on the old one (C1, above). Pull to make the join.

Or use this method instead:

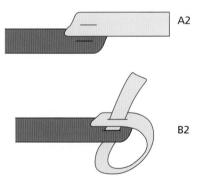

Align both strips and slits (A2, above).

Bring the unslit end of the top strip through both slits from the bottom—or the bottom strip through both slits from the top.

I rarely use either of these methods because they leave an untidy flap of fabric at the join, and because I often want a very precise color placement for intricate patterning. When I cut an existing weft at a specific place, I overlap the new strand inside the old one. Tapering one or both strips can reduce bulk at the join.

I don't recommend simply overlapping unjoined wefts or gluing them, although these are both options some people use.

Because joins are subject to wear if they're exposed at a selvedge, I try to position most joins within the twined rows. However, at the start of a project and for pattern changes, I prefer appearance over stability and may make a join deliberately at the selvedge.

Dealing with Raw Edges

Because knit fabrics don't ravel, their raw edges are not a problem. The edges of some knits will curl under as you work, although not always in the direction you prefer! If a knit fabric is printed or textured on only one side, you may have to manipulate strips to maintain the desired orientation.

If you're working with woven fabrics, you'll probably want to turn the raw edges under as you work to minimize the effect of raveling, discourage later raveling and produce a more pleasing appearance. While some rag twiners even press or sew under the edges before they start twining, this is more effort than I care to take. I try to fold edges under as I work. With narrow strips, you may only be able to fold them in half.

A printed fabric usually has a "wrong" side that's less attractive than the printed surface. In most cases, taking a little time to keep the "right" side out will produce a more pleasing project. Although projects worked in regular twining are usually reversible, the side you see as you work almost always looks better, and the reverse side may show the unprinted side of the fabric. Most napped fabric also has a "wrong" side. Orient the nap/grain in the same direction as you work to avoid streaks in the finished piece.

How Much Weft Do I Need?

Twining has considerable "take-up"; a certain length of weft will twine a shorter distance, up to 50 percent less. The heavier the fabric and warp and the wider the strip, the greater the take-up. The looser you twine, the more fabric it takes.

Sample ahead of time so you won't run out of fabric. Remember, twining uses two wefts (or more) at a time, so if 36" (91cm) of one weft twines 18" (46cm) of textile, you will need twice that amount (72" [183cm]) to twine the same distance (18" [46cm]) with two wefts.

Keep track of weft needs for your projects so you'll have a good estimate if you want to do something similar later. Count the number of strips as you cut them (also recording their length), then subtract any left over when you're done with your project.

If you have the fabric yardage and want to know how many strips you can get out of it, use the chart on this page to estimate. Amounts are rounded down to the nearest full yard. Where there is more than one figure, the appropriate one depends on which direction you'll be cutting the fabric.

If you know how many yards of strips you need (from the project instructions, for example), the chart below will help you determine the fabric yardage requirements. The formula is: Yardage Needed = Yards of Strips × (Strip Width ÷ Fabric Width).

Metric Conversion Chart

To convert	to	multiply by
Inches	Centimeters	2.54
Centimeters	Inches	0.4
Feet	Centimeters	30.5
Centimeters	Feet	0.03
Yards	Meters	0.9
Meters	Yards	1.1

Strip Yardage Yielded According to Strip Width

This table tells how many yards of strips a specific yardage of fabric will yield at different strip widths.

Fabric Width	Fabric Yardage	1"	1¼"	1½"	1¾"	2"	2¼"	2½"	2¾"	3"
36"	¼	9	7	6	5		4	3	3	3
36"	½	8	14	12	10	9	8	7	6	6
36"	¾	27	21	18	15	13	12	10	9	9
36"	1	36	28	24	20	18	16	14	13	12
44"	¼	11	8	7	6	4-5	4	3-4	3-4	3
44"	½	22	17	14	12	11	9	8	7-8	7
44"	¾	33	25-26	21-22	18	15-16	14	12	11-12	10-11
44"	1	44	35	29	25	22	19	17	16	14
65"	¼	16	12-13	109	7-8	7	5-6	5	-	5
65"	½	32	25-26	21	18	16	14	12-13	10-11	10
65"	¾	48	37-39	32	27	23-24	21	18-19	16-17	15-16
65"	1	65	50-52	43	36-37	32	28	25-26	23	21

Sources for Fabric

Traditionally, rag rugs were truly made with rags—worn-out clothing and other used fabrics. Today, it's perfectly okay to start with new yardage. Scraps left over from other projects are fine, too, especially if they're woven fabrics that don't have to be cut in a specific direction. I like to recycle sheets and some old clothing from thrift shops, where I also find fabric remnants. I sometimes plan a project around a colorful fabric I discover, or I may shop for new fabric to find just the color I have in mind.

Because twining uses considerable amounts of fabric, sometimes it's hard to find enough of a particular color in a remnant bin. Old sheets, bedspreads, thin blankets and draperies can provide ample quantities for certain projects.

Quilting stores provide wonderful inspiration for twining. Most quilt fabrics are cotton broadcloth or cotton blends. Fabric departments in discount stores often sell knit yardage at low prices. Some textile mills sell inexpensive selvedge remnants, sometimes already cut (although not always at the width you'll want). There are numerous mail-order sources for these mill ends.

Creative Fabric Recycling

An old seersucker shower curtain from a thrift shop was a wonderful match to my china, so I used it to make placemats and a runner.

Caring for Twined Projects

One reason twined rag rugs are so durable is because their warp is completely covered and protected. However, this is a disadvantage when it comes to cleaning.

Avoid soaking rugs and other densely twined items with rag warps; if the warp gets wet, it is difficult to dry, especially in humid climates. That can cause it to mildew or rot and make the twining fall apart.

Regular vacuuming (for a rug) and surface cleaning by hand without soaking are usually sufficient. For an item that will be subjected to moisture, choose a string warp that will dry more quickly than fabric or a synthetic cord that's impervious to moisture.

Some people machine-wash their twined rugs, although it makes the rugs wear out prematurely. Modern washers are tough on fabrics of all sorts—the reason our clothes wear out quickly is because we wash them so often! But not every twined project you make needs to last for generations, so if you choose to machine-wash your twined items, you should probably also machine-dry them to make sure the warp gets dry. Use gentle cycles.

Avoid beating or shaking a heavy twined item. A time-honored method of cleaning a rug, if you live in the proper climate, is to work dry snow into it and sweep it out before it melts.

Most lightweight projects in this book can be machine-washed (especially if constructed of knit fabric) or, for gentler handling, hand-washed as needed. Consider a spray-on stain repellant for items such as placemats that might need more frequent cleaning.

Chapter Three

Getting Started

Many newcomers to rag twining want to start a rug immediately. They quickly discover that it is a time-consuming process—especially when learning.

I recommend you start by twining a *Basic Twining Sampler (Hot Pad)* (page 38), which will give you all the experience you need to make larger projects, such as rugs, in a much shorter period of time. This one project incorporates the most common pattern techniques, and the finished sampler is a useful and attractive accessory for your kitchen. Later, as you twine other projects in this book, you'll want to use these instructions for reference on warping, starting, turning and finishing.

The *Basic Twining Sampler (Hot Pad)* incorporates three common patterns: checkerboard, horizontal stripes and vertical stripes. By the time you finish it, you will know more pattern techniques than 95 percent of the old-time rug twiners! Most of them used either the checkerboard pattern or vertical stripes; they didn't realize it took only a simple difference in turning at the side in order to make a striking pattern change. Very few of the old rug makers knew how to achieve each pattern deliberately.

If you've never twined with fabric before, please try this project before tackling the more complex ones found later in this book. Working with knit fabrics, which are easier to use, will help guarantee your success, especially if you choose fabrics of the same weight in two distinct colors.

Even after you've mastered rag twining, you'll find sampling on a small frame to be an excellent way of testing new fabric types and widths without using up a lot of material.

demonstration

countered twining

I recommend countered twining, where one row has the opposite pitch of the next, for rectangular pieces when it's important to keep the work flat. While you're learning, use wefts of compatible but distinct colors so you can easily tell them apart.

Here are diagrams for the most common pattern variations.

Twining Toward the Right

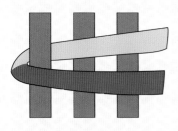

1 | START AT THE UPPER LEFT

Join 2 wefts of unequal length in different colors. Position the join at the upper left edge of the warp with 1 weft on top of the edge warp, the other underneath and then back to the surface. (Whenever a weft goes under a warp, it comes back to the surface immediately.) Extend the wefts horizontally toward the right.

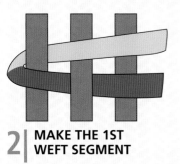

2 | MAKE THE 1ST WEFT SEGMENT

Bring the weft that's on top of the 1st warp down, below the other weft, under the 2nd warp, and back to the surface.

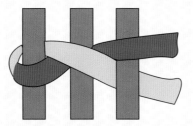

3 | TWINE THE 2ND WEFT SEGMENT

Take the weft on top of the 2nd warp, cross it over the other weft between the 2nd and 3rd warps (top to bottom), under the 3rd warp, and back to the surface.

Continue across, alternating wefts and always working with the weft that's farthest behind (in the direction you're working away from). Always cross the working weft over the other, top to bottom, and under the next warp. This crossing forms the half twist that creates the pitch (slant) distinctive of twining. Colors should alternate all the way across, and all weft segments in the 1st row should slant up to the left (left pitch).

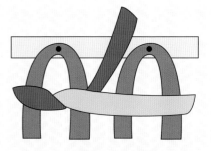

4 | PUT 1 WEFT UP OUT OF THE WAY

If you have trouble keeping the pitch consistent, take the weft that just went under a warp and put it up over the top of the frame, out of the way.

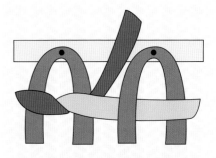

5 | TAKE THE OTHER WEFT UNDER THE NEXT WARP

Slip the remaining weft under the next warp.

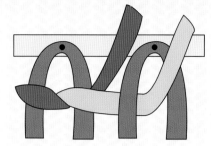

6 | PUT BOTH WEFTS UP

Put this 2nd weft up out of the way, parallel to the 1st weft. Don't allow them to cross at the top of the frame. Resume with the weft on the left.

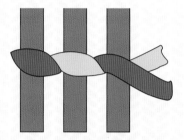

7 | ALTERNATE WEFTS, LEFT-PITCH TWINING

Twine to the end of the row, making sure 1 weft is on top of the right selvedge and the other weft underneath. Make sure wefts alternate all the way across; you have the same number of weft segments as warps and all segments have the same pitch.

Which Color's on Top?

Assuming you use both colors all the way across a row in regular twining, whether you start the turn with the same color that was on top of the first warp depends on whether you have an odd or an even number of warps. If an odd number, the same color will be on top of both left and right selvedge warps. If an even number, the colors will be different.

Always start the regular turn for countered twining with whichever weft is on top of the selvedge where you are turning.

Turning at the Right Side: Regular Turn

Of the several ways to turn at the side, I prefer the following methods because they best cover the warp on both sides.

I use the first option, the *regular turn* (below), for checkerboard patterns or whenever I'm working with two wefts of the same color. The second turn aligns colors vertically and is also used for taaniko twining (page 66). Both turns start the same.

The weft that starts on top of the first warp may or may not be the weft on top of the opposite selvedge warp, depending on whether you have an odd or an even number of warps. So pay less attention to the weft colors in the illustrations than to which weft is naturally on top when you start a turn.

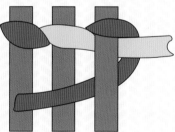

1 | START THE REGULAR TURN

Start with the weft on top of the right selvedge warp. Pass it behind the other weft, under the selvedge warp, and back to the surface between 1st and 2nd warps, headed left.

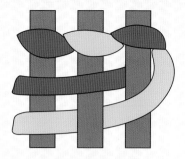

2 | FINISH THE TURN

Bring the 2nd weft over the selvedge warp, under the 2nd warp below the 1st weft, and back to the surface.

Twining Toward the Left

Continue twining toward the left, alternating wefts and always crossing them top to bottom as you did before. The twining direction (always toward the bottom or untwined warps) is the same, but the segments will slant up to the right (right pitch). This change in pitch is the countered twining that keeps your project from curling.

TWINE TOWARD THE LEFT

Work across to the left side. Weft colors (if you're using 2) should alternate both horizontally and vertically, creating a checkerboard pattern. All segments should have a right pitch, and there should be as many segments as you have warps.

Turning at the Left

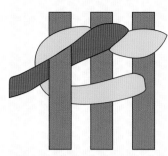

1 | START THE TURN

Make the turn the same way as at the right side. Start with the weft on top of the selvedge warp, carry it behind the other weft and under the selvedge warp, then back to the surface heading right.

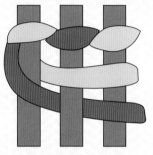

2 | FINISH THE TURN

Bring the 2nd weft over the selvedge warp, then under the 2nd warp, keeping the 1st weft above it.

Alternate Turn: Right Side

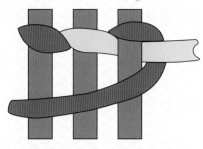

1 | KEEP THE SAME WEFT ON TOP

This turn keeps the same color on top of the selvedge to start the next row. Start with the weft on top of the selvedge warp, carry it behind the 2nd weft, then back over the selvedge to start the next row. Do not put it under the next warp yet!

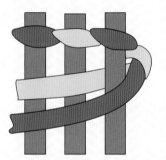

2 | COMPLETE THE TURN

Bring the 2nd weft under the selvedge warp and back to the surface between 1st and 2nd warps, keeping it above the 1st weft.

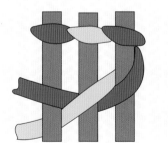

3 | START THE NEXT ROW

Twine toward the left, crossing the 2nd weft over the 1st, top to bottom, and under the 3rd warp. A little of the 2nd weft may show at the right edge. Gently pull it at the 2nd segment until it disappears.

Twist Toward the Untwined Warps

If you're strongly right- or left-handed, you may find one twining or twist direction more natural than the other when you are first learning. You also may find turning at one side easier than at the other.

The left-pitch twining shown for the first row is more natural for a left-handed person, but it makes more sense to twist toward the untwined ("open") warp than toward the top of the frame or the previous row; doing so helps pack rows together.

Once you have a little experience and can keep the pitch constant within a row, both directions should begin to feel equally comfortable.

Alternate Turn: Left Side

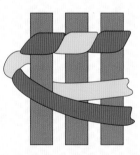

ALTERNATE TURN AT THE LEFT

The alternate turn is the same at the left as at the right. Start with the weft on top of the selvedge, take it behind the other weft, and bring it over the selvedge to start the next row. The 2nd weft comes under the selvedge, then crosses over the other weft and under the 3rd warp.

equipment and materials

- Sampler frame (see page 11) 11" × 11" (28cm x 28cm) outside dimension (7½"[19cm] inside) with 8 brads spaced at 1" (25mm) intervals across both the top and bottom
- Warp and weft materials (see page 39)
- 2 safety pins
- Sewing needle
- Thread to match project fabrics
- Scissors
- Rotary fabric cutter (optional)
- Cutting mat (optional)
- Medium crochet hook (F, G or H)

basic twining sampler (hot pad)

By the time you finish this hot pad, you will know more pattern techniques than most rug twiners ever learned! The majority of rug makers twined simple random or striped designs, either with the checkerboard variation that starts this sampler or the vertical columns in its center—but few people knew how to do both patterns deliberately. Although the only difference is how you turn at the edge, the pattern change is astonishing.

   I recommend knit fabrics for your first sampler; the raveling from woven fabric can interfere with the learning process. The fabric warp and relatively wide weft strips are appropriate for rugs and other projects requiring heavy, durable results.

Finished size: 8¼" tall × 7½" wide (21cm × 19cm).

Warp: Light blue knit cut 1¼" (3cm) wide—4 yards (4m) sewn into a continuous strip.

Wefts:
- Dark blue knit cut 1¼" (3cm) wide—7 yards (6m).
- Light blue knit (same fabric as the warp) cut
    1¼" (3cm) wide—8 yards (7m).

Warping Method: Continuous.

Number of Warps: 15.

Warp Spacing: 2 per inch (25mm).

Number of Weft Rows: 21.

Weft Spacing: 2½ rows per inch (25mm).

Twining Method: Countered twining.

Project Notes

Throughout this book, the lengths refer to the number of yards (meters) of strips, not total fabric yardage unless otherwise stated.

Fabric Samples

Choose knit fabrics of the same medium weight that are distinct but compatible in color—either two solids or a solid and a patterned fabric that you can tell apart easily when they are twisted together.

I used the light blue fabric for warp as well as weft.

Warping

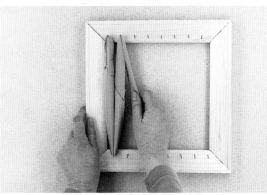

1 | DO THE WARPING

At the upper left corner, loop 1 end of the warp around the 1st nail, allowing 2–3" (5–8cm) overlap. Pin it temporarily.

Zigzag the warp between the nails, top to bottom, keeping the strands taut and the tension consistent, but not as tight as possible.

End at the lower right corner; loop the warp around the last nail and pin it in place. Do not cut off the excess warp.

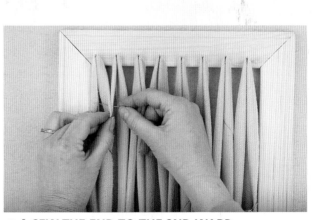

2 | SEW THE END TO THE 2ND WARP

Remove the pin; sew the end to the 2nd warp. As you twine, treat the entire end strand as part of the 2nd warp.

Join wefts; position the join at the left selvedge, dark weft on top of 1st warp, light weft under. Bring the light weft to the surface, right, parallel and a bit above the dark weft. Work 1" (25mm) from the top.

Twining

First Segment
The dark weft will be the first segment.

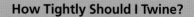

How Tightly Should I Twine?

A rug designed for hard use will last longest if you twine densely by pulling wefts tightly and packing the rows firmly. However, the same tightness might be less appropriate for a table mat, where some flexibility and less density is desirable. The projects in this book range from sturdy rugs meant to be walked on to lightweight textiles. A given pattern may dictate a specific spacing for the warps, weft segments and weft rows in order to achieve the desired results.

1 | THE 1ST TWINING MOTION
Bring the dark weft down, under the 2nd warp and back to the surface, including the end of the 1st warp as part of the 2nd.

3 | PUT THE DARK WEFT OUT OF THE WAY
Twine across, alternating wefts and colors. If you are confused, put the weft you just passed under a warp up over the top of the frame (dark weft shown here).

2 | FORM THE 2ND SEGMENT (LIGHT)
Cross the light weft over the dark, top to bottom; pass it under the 3rd warp and back to the surface.

4 | WORK WITH THE LIGHT WEFT, THEN THE DARK
Slip the light weft under the next warp.

5 | TWINE WITH THE OTHER WEFT
Put the light weft up, parallel to the dark weft without crossing it, and bring the dark weft down and under the next warp.

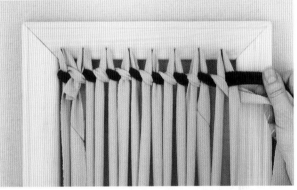

6 | THE END OF THE 1ST ROW
Finish the 1st row and make sure colors alternate, all segments have a left pitch and you have as many segments as warps.

7 | START THE REGULAR TURN
Start the regular turn with the weft on top at the selvedge. Bring it behind the other weft, under the selvedge and back to the surface between the first 2 warps.

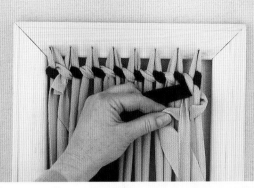

8 | COMPLETE THE TURN
Bring the other weft over the selvedge warp, then under the 2nd warp, below the 1st weft.

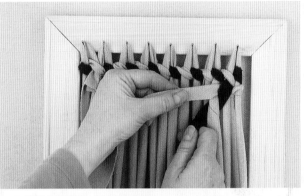

9 | START THE 2ND ROW
Continue twining as before, always crossing wefts top to bottom and toward the bottom of the frame. Colors should alternate vertically and horizontally to form the checkerboard pattern, and all segments in the 2nd row should have a right pitch.

10 | MOVE THE ROWS UPWARD
Finish the 2nd row and move both rows tight against the nails (pull on warp pairs as you push weft rows). Evaluate these rows. If segments are too bulky and the warp bulges, cut strips narrower, twine tighter or eliminate a warp pair. If the warp pulls in at the sides or shows within rows, widen the wefts or twine looser. With a larger project, if your equipment allows, add or subtract warps if it doesn't interfere with your pattern.

11| SECURE AND TRIM THE END OF THE WARP

Once you are happy with the weft widths and the number of warps, rotate the frame (top to bottom), sew the end of the warp to the adjacent warp, as at the start, and cut off the excess.

14| JOINING A NEW WEFT TO THE OLD ONE

When you run short of weft, attach another piece of the same color (as long as your pattern is not changing).

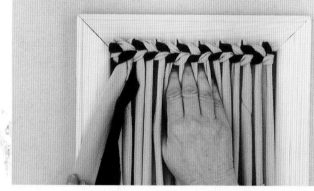

12| CHECK FOR CROSSED WARPS

Start 2 new warps in the upper left, with the same (dark) color with which you started the other end on top of the selvedge. Twine 1 or 2 rows in checkerboard pattern. Slide your fingers up and down between warps to make sure you haven't crossed any; if you have, retwine 1 end or the other in the correct order.

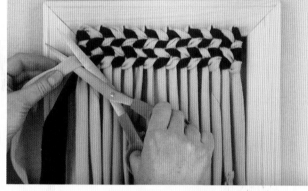

15| CUT THE TOP WEFT RIGHT AT THE EDGE

At the end of the 4th row, cut the light weft at the selvedge.

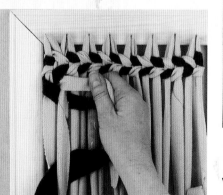

13| COMPLETE THE REGULAR TURN

Continue from either end. Use a regular turn at the left selvedge, just as at the right, starting with the weft on top of the selvedge.

16| SEW A DARK WEFT TO THE LIGHT ONE

Untwine a few segments and attach a dark weft to the end of the light weft. A sewn join makes the most precise color change; sew the new weft inside the old one.

17| **START THE SOLID STRIPE**
Retwine the end of the 4th row, use a regular turn and continue twining with 2 dark wefts. Since you won't have a color alternation, be careful to maintain the same number of segments with the correct pitch.

19| **SEWING A LIGHT WEFT INSIDE THE DARK END**
Untwine a few segments and attach a light weft to the dark weft you just cut.

18| **ENDING THE DARK STRIPE**
Twine 2 solid dark rows. Cut the weft that's underneath the left selvedge.

20| **START THE ALTERNATE TURN**
Retwine to the end of the row and use the alternate turn to keep the dark weft on top, passing it behind the light weft and keeping it on the surface.

Working From Both Ends

It's traditional to twine from both ends of a rug (or other rectangular project) and end closer to the center, occasionally rotating the frame top to bottom. Especially with fabric warps, twining the rows at both ends helps align the warps and makes crossed warps less likely. It's also physically easier to finish the last row away from the sides of the frame and the nails or wires. Ending in the middle of a row is more secure than ending at a selvedge.

It's not necessary to rotate a frame constantly or to end exactly in the center. When working intricate patterns, I prefer to end a project in a background area, and I may work most of a pattern from the top down and end a few rows up from the bottom.

21| **COMPLETE THE TURN**
Take the light weft under the selvedge warp.

22 | COMPLETE THE 2ND SEGMENT

Cross the dark weft over the light between the first 2 warps, and bring the dark weft under the 2nd warp. The light strand goes under the 3rd warp.

23 | HIDING THE LIGHT WEFT AT THE SIDE

If the light weft shows at the edge, gently pull it to hide it.

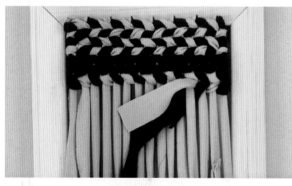

24 | MAKING VERTICAL STRIPES

Continue twining with both colors, using the alternate turn at both sides to align the colors vertically. Work from both ends toward the center, using the same patterning on each end. Finish the sampler in the center section (not necessarily the exact center), on the inside of a row and away from the sides of the frame. The last row must have the opposite pitch from the row above and below it. My sampler has 9 center rows; yours may have more or fewer, but it will be an odd number. The 4 wefts will come together at the end.

Pattern Techniques

The projects that follow incorporate some of the many other twining techniques for creating interesting patterns. I'll introduce them in the instructions.

25 | SEWING THE LAST SEGMENT

Punch 2 same-color wefts to the back of the sampler, covering the warp as if you were completing a weft segment. Pull the 2 wefts together on each side to form the last segments; sew them together near the sampler surface.

26 | SECURING THE ENDS

Cut a small slit near the end of each weft; use a crochet hook to pull each vertically through 3 or 4 rows, parallel to an adjacent warp. For each pair, pull 1 up, 1 down beside different warps to minimize bulk.

Trim the ends close to the surface to hide them. Slip the warp off the nails. Your sampler is finished!

demonstration

speeding the process

By the time you've finished your first sampler, you should be comfortable with all the basic techniques, and you should no longer have to put wefts up out of the way to maintain the proper pitch. As you gain experience, you will probably modify your hand positions to make twining efficient and rhythmic.

Here is the way I work, shown on the placemat project (page 93) with a string warp.

1 | PASSING THE WEFT TO THE LEFT HAND

My right hand holds both wefts and passes the working weft to the left hand.

2 | PUTTING THE WEFT UNDER THE NEXT WARP

My left hand pushes the weft under the next warp.

3 | PULLING THE WEFT THROUGH

My right hand releases the other weft and pulls the working weft to the surface, while my left hand packs the segments up against the previous row.

Some people find it more natural to work from the bottom of the frame upwards, or sideways. Except as noted, all diagrams and photos in this book assume you work from the top down, so you may need to turn the diagrams to suit your preferred method. (Instructions for the *Argyle Rug* on page 61, Chapter Four provide diagrams for working from the bottom up.)

How Long Does Twining Take?

Like most hand-manipulated crafts, twining requires some time. When you work on a project that requires many weft segments, you will develop a pleasing rhythm that makes the time pass quickly. Although a rug or finely twined project may take many hours, by comparison twining is not as time-consuming as quilting. A moderate-size rug may take twenty to thirty hours, including time for fabric preparation, depending on the complexity of the pattern.

One benefit of twining is you don't have to set aside lengthy work periods. You can twine a row or a few segments in your spare time and be ready to continue whenever you come back to it.

"Challenges" to Watch For
This small sampler incorporates many undesirable features.

How Do I Fix This?

What some people call mistakes and problems, I prefer to call "design elements" and "challenges." Although some interesting patterns can result from creative experimentation, you will probably encounter some results that don't please you.

Here's a troubleshooting guide to help you diagnose and remedy these situations. When you get to the point where you can identify your "design elements," you're making progress!

Undesirable Features

(A) There are more weft segments than warps. Twine the entire end of the warp together with the second warp.

(B) One weft is looser and shows more than the other. Tug on the weft that shows more (here, the light weft) to equalize the tension.

(C) The dark weft crossed the light weft vertically, between warps, resulting in adjacent light segments. The dark weft shows as an extra segment without pitch. Make sure wefts alternate on the surface of the warps.

(D) Improper regular turn. Carry the dark weft all the way to the edge before the turn. The last warp must have one weft beneath it and the other on top.

(E) Two segments have no pitch; the wefts didn't cross each other and the warp shows. Be sure to cross wefts between each pair of warps.

(F) The pitch changes. Cross wefts consistently within a row, keeping the working weft below the other.

(G) Improper regular turn. Start the turn with the weft that lies on top of the selvedge warp.

(H) One segment enclosed two warps or skipped a warp. (A skipped warp will show on the back side.) Each row needs the same number of segments as warps.

(I) Two adjacent dark segments. The dark weft was sewn outside the end of the light weft instead of inside it. Enclose the new weft inside the old one.

(J) Improper alternate turn. The dark weft went under the second warp before the light weft came under the selvedge, resulting in the wrong pitch. Also, the light weft shows at the edge; pull it gently to hide it (see also M, this page).

(K) The warp shows at the turn. This is normal; the alternate turn was correct. Pack rows more closely to minimize this effect.

(L) This was the last row. To the left (seventh warp from the right), wefts of both colors were sewn together, and the two ends were pulled the wrong directions into the sampler to hide them. The last segments should show the normal pitch. To the right (sixth warp from the right), the warp shows because the remaining wefts were taken to the back side without covering the warp. Light wefts should have covered this warp.

(M) The warp shows because wefts were not cut to balance. The light weft is too narrow compared to the dark weft. Also, the light weft shows at the selvedge (see also J, this page).

(N) The sides pull in and the warp shows. Both wefts are too narrow. Twine more loosely or (better) cut strips wider.

(O) The warp is distorted outwards because both wefts are too bulky. Cut narrower strips and/or twine more tightly.

(P) The corner curls because the bottom two rows have the same pitch (the last row has the incorrect pitch). Avoid same-pitch twining on the ends of a project.

(Q) The warp shows at the top and bottom edges. Choose a warp the same color as one of the wefts in the top and bottom rows. Because of the striking color difference between warp and wefts, the warp also shows through on the surface between rows, even where the twining is correct.

(R) The wefts have slipped off the selvedge warp because the end of the warp was looped around the nail and sewn to itself. Be sure to sew the end of the warp to the adjacent warp. Otherwise you must sew the weft to the warp in that corner.

A Different Set of "Challenges"
The emphasis in this unfinished sampler is on warp and fabric challenges.

Warp and Fabric Challenges

(1) The raveled edges of a denim warp show through on the surface, detracting from the elegant look of a smooth nylon weft. Avoid this kind of texture contrast between warp and weft.

(2) Although twined correctly in checkerboard pattern, the pattern doesn't show. The plaid weft is too close in color to the alternating solid pink. Choose compatible, but more distinct colors. A fabric with changing colors will tend to obscure any deliberate pattern.

(3) This loosely woven twill fabric ravels readily, making it difficult to work with and unstable for many projects. Avoid this type of fabric unless you want this textured effect. Cutting strips with a rotary cutter will help minimize raveling.

(4) The wrong side of this printed fabric shows on the surface. One reason the back side of your work usually isn't as attractive as the front is because you have less control over the fabric you don't see as you're working. Manipulate wefts carefully, and turn under raw edges as you work to keep the right side out.

(5) Wefts are unequal in elasticity. The stretchier weft is not as visible, and some of its segments appear to have little pitch. The more elastic weft has pulled in the edges. Choose fabrics of similar elasticity, or twine the stretchier fabric loosely without pulling it.

(6) Both wefts are too stretchy—the selvedges are pulled inward. Avoid stretchy wefts or twine them very carefully without pulling them.

(7) Weft segments have folds or creases. The twisting and compression of twining make it difficult to keep all segments looking smooth. Turning raw edges under equally on each side of the strip creates a better look; however, the creased effect is part of the nature of fabric twining. The third row is a little smoother because of more careful attention to turning edges under.

(8) These warps are crossed. Twining both ends, then checking for crossed warps helps avoid this situation, catching it when it's easy to make a correction. If you don't locate crossed warps until you're well into a project, disguise the problem by packing rows firmly.

(9) This warp has broken. Splice a broken warp by pulling the ends together tightly, overlapping if possible, and sewing the ends together.

(10) This warp is too loose. Sew a tuck in it to tighten it.

Notes About the Projects

The warp and weft amounts included in the project instructions call for a certain number of yards—which always refers to the number of yards of fabric strips needed, *not* to the yardage of the original fabric! Refer to the tables on pages 32 and 140.

For example, a project that requires 36 yards (33m) of strips 1" (25mm) wide would use a square yard of fabric, *not* 36 yards of original fabric. If the strips need to be 2¼" (6cm) wide, you'll get 16 strips from one square yard of fabric; it would take 2¼ yards (2m) of fabric to give you 36 wider (2¼" [6cm]) strips.

In most cases, the instructions add approximately ten percent to the lengths I used in the actual projects, to allow for differences in fabric and twining habits. It's always a good idea to have more fabric available than you think you'll need.

Substituting Fabrics

The project instructions list the specific warp materials, fabrics and colors I used. It's unlikely you'll locate the same fabrics, so you'll have to substitute your own. Choose similar weights and types to get similar results, but don't be afraid to use knits where I've used woven fabrics and vice versa.

You can substitute hardware string for crochet yarn or whatever you have available in about the same size. The projects are simply guidelines for your own twining, and creativity is encouraged!

Be sure to cut all knits in the direction of least stretch, and if your fabrics are heavier or lighter than mine, cut them at appropriate widths.

New warping and pattern techniques are introduced as they appear in the project. I've recommended specific equipment, but many of the rectangular projects can be twined on other sorts of frames.

Your Results May Differ

Sometimes when I finished a project, I decided if I ever did it again I'd make some changes. Therefore, I've incorporated some minor changes in the instructions so your projects can turn out better than mine; in a few cases the row-by-row instructions may give slightly different results from what you see in the photos.

Develop the confidence to change the directions as needed, perhaps adding more or fewer warps, adding warps at a different place or even changing the patterns themselves. Only the rectangular diamond rugs require a precise spacing and number of rows; and even with those, you can add or subtract rows as long as you follow the correct color sequence and alter the graphs to maintain symmetry.

If you are designing your own projects, keep track of the amount of fabric for future reference. After sampling a row or two to make sure I'm satisfied with the widths of weft and warp strips, I cut multiple strips and record the total length. As I need to add more, I record their lengths also. If any are left over at the end of the project, I subtract them to determine the total yardage needed.

Chapter Four

Twining Rugs on Tensioned Warps

For more than a century, creative rug makers, many with limited resources, have twined beautiful, sturdy rugs on inexpensive frames with warps under tension. The majority of these rugs have had variegated (*hit-and-miss*) patterns or simple stripes. Few twiners knew they could accomplish more pattern excitement with only a little more effort and planning, as today's rug twiners worldwide are discovering.

Weavers with conventional looms generally use faster weaving methods to make rag rugs, few of which can match twined rugs for durability and the potential for intricate patterning. Nevertheless, floor looms are also practical for twining, permitting tension adjustment, long warps and a comfortable working position. A loom functions like a horizontal frame for twining. If you have a loom, try twining a rug on it. This chapter will tell you how.

The designs in this section range from simple classic patterns to exciting modern variations combining the best of twining traditions with intricate patterning. Most, even with complex-looking designs, are easy enough for beginners, and a few rows of practice will make anyone an expert! There are also challenges (*A Child's Sleeping Mat* and *Toe Tickler Rug*) for those with more experience.

Join today's twiners who are discovering the excitement of rugs such as these. Use either a frame or a loom to make any of these stunning creations!

equipment and materials

- Frame with suspended wires or pegs, at least 24" × 36" (61cm × 91cm)
- Warp and weft materials (see page 52)
- 2 safety pins
- Sewing needle
- Thread to match project fabrics
- Scissors
- Rotary fabric cutter (optional)
- Cutting mat (optional)
- Medium crochet hook (F, G or H)

hit-and-miss rug

Since they were made from whatever scraps were available (usually in small quantities), traditional hit-and-miss woven rugs combined a rainbow of colors, textures and fabrics. Twining hit-and-miss fashion adds even more color excitement than weaving, since you can use two different weft colors at once, producing spots of color to brighten your floor. This rug uses a limited range of colors—browns and oranges—to better fit a particular home color scheme.

Finished Size: 35" long × 24" wide (89cm × 61cm)—1" (25mm) shorter than the on-the-frame measurement, to compensate for a little stretch in the warp.

Warp: Heavy dark brown knit fabric cut 1¼" (3cm) wide—48½ yards (44m) of warp.

Wefts: 13 knit fabrics, orange and brown solids and prints, in varying weights. For the photographed project, the strips were cut to balance, 1¼–2¼" (3cm–6cm). Total weft, approximately 183 yards (167m), 10–16 yards (9m–15m) of each.

Warping Method: Warp loops.

Number of Warps: 48 (24 loops).

Warp Spacing: 2 per inch (25mm).

Number of Weft Rows: 73.

Weft Spacing: 2 rows per inch (25mm).

Twining Method: Countered twining.

Putting Warp Loops on a Pegged Frame
Stretch warp loops between pegs or suspended wires, staggering the joins.

Fabric Samples
Knit fabrics are practical for a rug that won't ravel during or after construction. These fabrics are of different weights, cut to balance. The dark brown warp fabric is also used for weft.

Warping

1 | **PREPARE THE WARP LOOPS**
To compensate for the minor stretching that occurs when the warps are under tension, make each warp 35" (89cm) long. Fold 2 yards (2m) of fabric in half and stitch 1" (25mm) from the ends, reinforcing with another row of stitching on top of the first. The stitching is perpendicular to the warpwise direction of least stretch.

2 | **CUT**
Cut the loops.

Twining

1 PREPARE THE WEFTS

For the best color excitement, use wefts about ½ yard (46cm) to 1 yard (91cm) long, so that the colors change frequently. You can sew short strips together by machine before you start twining, if you wish.

2 TWINE LEFT TO RIGHT

Start twining with 2 different weft colors from the upper left, using 1 weft the same color as the warp and staggering the ends. Work in regular countered twining, using the regular turn at the selvedges.

4 ROTATE THE FRAME

After a row or 2, rotate the frame top to bottom and start with 2 new wefts (1 the same as the warp) at the upper left. Check for crossed warps and continue from either end. Rotate the frame occasionally to work toward the center.

Choose weft colors in a pleasing order. Although the effect of this rug is random color placement, I actually deliberate which color to choose whenever I need to attach a new weft. I try to avoid large areas of dark wefts or light wefts and distribute the brighter fabrics throughout, balancing the use of solids and prints. There's no need to use the same colors in the same order at each end of the rug.

5 FINISH THE FRAME

End anywhere away from the edges of the frame (it does not have to be in the center), maintaining countered twining. Remove the rug from the frame. Sew wefts together to form the last segments and use the crochet hook to pull the ends alongside the warps, hidden within several rows of twining. Trim the ends.

3 SNUG THE SEGMENTS UP

Move the 1st row tight against the pegs or wire to minimize loops at the end of the warps.

Bar Feature
On this frame, a bar offers protection from the pegs and keeps the warp from slipping off.

"Diamond" Rugs

In recent years, rag rug weavers have been experimenting with "diamond" rug patterning. When a color repeat (the length of a regular sequence of colors that repeats itself in a project) is slightly longer or slightly shorter than the width of the rug, the colors shift a little with each row to produce predictable, argyle-like patterning. Similarly with twining, if the number of weft segments in a color repeat is slightly more or slightly fewer than the number of segments in the rug width, a shifting pattern results. The effect looks much more complicated than it really is.

In a twined rug, best results come when the color repeat and rug width are only one segment different, and when you have the same number of segments (warps) per inch (25mm) as weft rows per inch (25mm). Sampling determines the ideal length of each weft strip in order to twine the desired number of segments. Then, careful attention to counting segments and maintaining a consistent row and warp spacing is all that's needed to achieve spectacular results.

Planning a Twined Diamond Rug

You are not limited to two or three colors, or a balanced (or near-balanced) number of segments of each color, like those in the following projects. Experiment with other color and segment sequences and more color variation. The number of warps can be either odd or even, the color repeat either one fewer or one more segment than the number of warps. Innovative weavers are achieving curved patterns in their rugs by slightly and gradually changing the length of the color repeat within a project, something else you can try with twining.

If you are not using the full length of your warp in a rug (for example, if you desire to leave some warp as fringe or plan to weave in the warp ends by hand), it's not always necessary to graph a design ahead of time, as long as you're sure you'll have extra warp length. However, for a four-selvedge rug, using colored pencils or markers on graph paper will assure you know in advance just how many rows you'll need to achieve a relatively symmetrical pattern. Computer graphing software, designed for needleworkers and weavers, makes the designing process faster, but you can do it by hand just as successfully. Use a zigzag pattern, left to right and then right to left for the next row, in the same manner you'd use to twine back and forth.

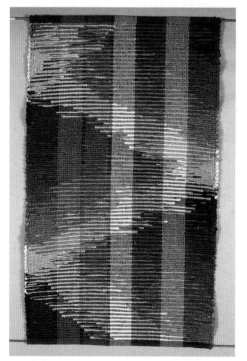

A Woven *Diamond* Rug
A mathematical formula creates the shifting patterns.
Kathy's Garden #4, *designed and woven by Debra K. Sharpee, DeForest, Wisconsin; photo courtesy of Debra K. Sharpee.*

A Twined *Diamond* Rug
Wilma Nelsen of Custer, Michigan, twined this rug using consistent lengths of four colors of fabric. *Rug from the collection of Bobbie Irwin; photo by Bobbie Irwin.*

equipment and materials

- Frame with suspended wires or pegs 36" (91cm) apart, at least 24" (61cm) wide
- Warp and weft materials (see page 56)
- Sewing needle
- Thread to match project fabrics
- Scissors
- Rotary fabric cutter (optional)
- Cutting mat (optional)
- Medium crochet hook (F, G or H)

aurora rug

Amaze your friends with this dramatic two-color rug that reminds me of the northern lights shifting in the night sky. I made this four-selvedge rug on a frame, with two segments and rows per inch (25mm). Maintaining consistent row spacing is the trickiest part, necessary to keep the diagonals at the ideal 45-degree angle. Since you need to twine from both ends and end up with a predetermined number of rows, pay careful attention to the number of rows per inch (25mm) as you work.

Finished Size: 36" long × 24" wide (91cm × 61cm)—½" (13mm) shorter than the graphed design because of a little stretch in the warp.

Warp: Medium-weight knit fabrics.
-Turquoise cut 1¾" (4cm) wide—47 yards (43m).
-Navy cut 2" (5cm) wide—46 yards (42m).

Weft: Same as the warp fabrics, cut the same widths—84 yards (77m) of turquoise strips, 76 yards (69m) of navy strips.

Warping Method: Warp loops.
To compensate for the minor stretching that occurs when the warps are under tension, make each warp 35" (89cm) long. Except for the 4 center warps (see below), cut each strip 36" (91cm) long and sew with a ½" (13mm) seam allowance to make the loops.

Number of Warps: 48 (24 loops). You need 44 loops that are half turquoise, half navy; and 2 loops with slightly more turquoise (more than 36" [91cm]) than navy.

Warp Spacing: 2 per inch (25mm).

Number of Weft Rows: 73.

Weft Spacing: 2 rows per inch (25mm).

Warping

1 | PLACE WARPS ON WIRES OR PEGS

On the graph, note the color of the wefts in the top and bottom rows. The warp colors here should match the wefts.

For example, the first 11 warp pairs (1 loop makes a pair) from left to right are turquoise at the top and navy at the bottom—the reverse of the 11 pairs from the right toward the center. The single warp just left of center needs to be all turquoise, attached to a warp that's turquoise at the top and navy at the bottom; position a color change at the lower end.

The warp just right of center is also all turquoise, attached to a warp that's navy at the top and turquoise at the bottom.

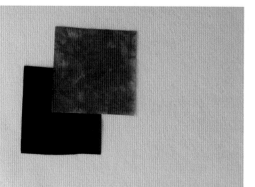

Fabric Samples
Knit fabrics are practical for a rug that won't ravel during or after construction. These are of slightly different weights; the lighter-weight fabric (navy) is cut slightly wider.

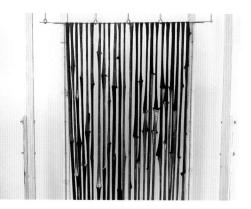

2 | ROTATE THE LOOPS SO SEAMS ARE NOT ALIGNED

Position warps so the colors match the top and bottom rows of the graph, with seams staggered to minimize bulk.

Twining

1 | WORK WITH TURQUOISE WEFTS

With each pair, twine the warp on the front side of the wire before the warp on the back side. Start at the upper left, an inch (25mm) or so down from the top, with a single strand of turquoise weft at least 40" (102cm) long. Measure and record the exact length of the unstretched fabric.

Fold the strip in half to form 2 wefts, positioning the fold at the left selvedge. It's not necessary to stagger the ends because both wefts will be cut at the same place in the row.

If using a frame with wires, twine each warp pair in the same order, starting with the warp on either the front or the back side of the wire each time. The choice is yours, but be consistent.

Twine exactly 25 segments with turquoise wefts. Cut both wefts between the 25th and 26th warps (counted from the left). Measure the amount of fabric that remains and subtract from the original length to determine how much you used. Half that measurement, plus the amount of overlap you use when joining new wefts, will be the amount needed for each turquoise weft. Sewn joins are best for the abrupt and precise color changes needed in diamond rugs.

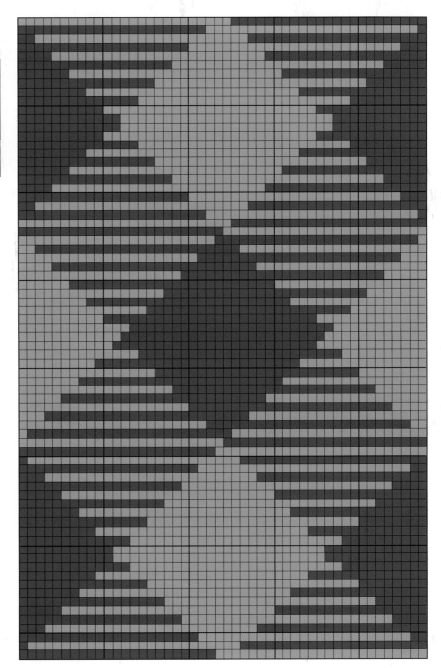

Graph for *Aurora Rug*

As long as you maintain a consistent number of segments per color (25 turquoise, 24 navy), you do not need to keep track of each row in the graph; the pattern should develop naturally.

Reading a Graph

A twining graph shows the color for each weft segment. Each square in a graph represents one weft segment covering one warp. Each column of squares represents a single warp, and each horizontal row shows one row of twining. The lines between the squares are not warps or wefts.

2 | WORK WITH NAVY WEFTS

Cut 2 measured navy wefts, each at least 20" (51cm) long, and attach them to the ends of the turquoise. Sewing the navy inside the turquoise gives accurate color positioning (important to achieve the diamond pattern).

Twine 24 segments of navy, using the regular turn and ending after the 1st segment on the 2nd row. If using wire selvedge guides, twine around both the selvedge warp and the wire together, treating the wire as part of the warp. Make sure you maintain a consistent 2 warps/weft segments per inch (25mm).

Subtract the remaining navy strip lengths from the original lengths to get a good estimate for cutting future strips with minimal waste. Attach turquoise wefts.

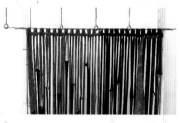

3 | START THE 2ND ROW WITH TURQUOISE WEFTS

In countered twining, twine 25 turquoise segments, right to left, then 24 navy segments. Maintain a row spacing of 2 per inch (25mm).

Count the appropriate number of segments for each color as you work. The pattern shifts 1 segment per color per row. After twining 2 rows, move the rows up tight against the wires or pegs.

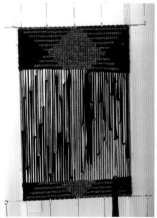

4 | TWINE BOTH ENDS

Twine both ends of the rug using the same color sequence, as shown on the graph. Rotate the frame, bottom to top, and twine the opposite end in the same manner, starting left to right (because the pattern calls for an odd number of rows). Rotate the graph as well; the color sequence is the same, 25 turquoise segments followed by 24 navy.

Twine a row, making sure you keep the warps in the same order as at the other end; check for crossed warps, and make any needed corrections. Continue working from either or both ends.

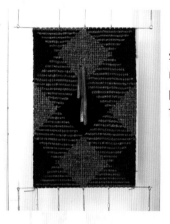

5 | FINISH THE RUG

End the rug in any solid color area, within a row and away from the pegs, wires or sides of the frame.

6 | TAKE THE RUG OFF THE FRAME

Make sure the last row has the opposite slant of the row above and below, and that you have the required number of total rows (73).

Pull and sew wefts together to form the last segments; poke 1 pair to the back side. With the crochet hook, pull weft ends vertically through several rows either above or below the last row. Cut off the excess. If using a frame with wires, pull out the top, bottom and selvedge wires to remove the rug.

Twining on a Standard Loom

Historically, few weavers with floor looms made twined rugs because they could weave other types much faster. So it doesn't make sense to buy a loom for twining rugs—unless you really need an excuse to explore the wonderful world of weaving as well!

However, if you already have a loom, there's no reason not to use it for twining. While there's no speed advantage, it does make working comfortable, allows tension control and is especially practical for long rugs and runners that might not fit as well on a frame. The length is limited only by the amount of finished rug you can wind around the cloth beam of your loom.

It's easy to use your favorite warping method and twine a rug with fringed ends. You also have the option of finishing the ends by pulling the warps back through the rug by hand.

You can twine a four-selvedge rug on most looms without requiring any special finishing. Ironically this is trickier on a standard loom than on a simple frame!

Standard Loom

Preparing the Loom

The loom in the photo uses a pulley system to raise the heddle frames (shafts). Here, I removed the frames and tied back the pulley cords so I could easily hang the frames later without having to reconfigure the entire pulley system. I've also removed the entire beater and extended the back rod as far forward as it will come.

During twining, there's no need for heddles or treadles because you don't raise or lower the warps as you do in weaving. Remove the heddle frames if possible, tying the heddles to the sides (if the loom's weaving width is wider than your rug project).

If you're making a fringed rug or plan to weave the warps back in, you can use the beater and a coarse-dent reed to pack the weft rows. For this four-selvedge rug, remove the reed.

Warping for a Four-Selvedge Rug

For a four-selvedge rug, twine from both the front and back of the loom in order to work toward the center.

Before you start warping, extend the back rod as far forward as it will come. Measure the distance from the rod through the castle to about 12" (30cm) from the front beam (toward the castle). If your loom is small, with less than 12" (30cm) between the front beam and castle, measure the distance from the back rod to about 2" (5cm) in front of the castle. You will need to twine this distance from the back of the loom in order to end the rug comfortably from the front side.

If your planned project is shorter than the distance between the breast and back beams, wind a continuous warp. Tie stiff wire to the back and front rods, leaving space to wind the warp around the wires. Attach the end of the warp to the adjacent (not same) warp.

Use a figure-eight warping technique: bottom to top over the front wire, then bottom to top over the back wire. The warps cross at the center of the loom, forming the *weaver's cross* that keeps them in order.

It's easier to use warp loops for a warp of any length. Loop them around a wire that you then secure tightly right against the back rod. Insert a second wire in the loops and pull it forward. Wind the warps onto the warp beam (if the warp is long enough) and tie the front wire closely to the front rod. Tension with the normal loom tensioning system.

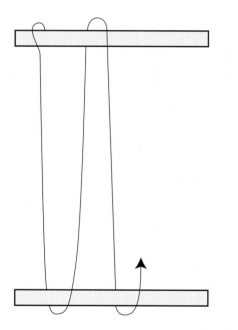

Winding a Figure-Eight Warp

Twining Toward the Top

When you twine on a loom, work from the bottom up, crossing wefts away from you toward the un-twined warp.

I start at the left side with right pitch; you could start at the right with left pitch.

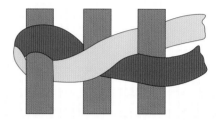

(A) Starting Twining, Working from the Bottom Up

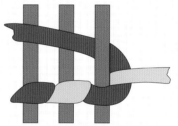

(B) Starting the Regular Turn

(C) Completing the Turn

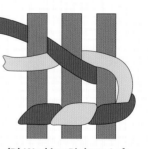

(D) Working Right to Left in Countered Twining

(E) Turning at the Left Side

equipment and materials

- Standard loom with a weaving width of at least 22" (56cm), or any frame that will fit the project dimensions
- 2 straight wires at least 24" (61cm) long
- Twist ties or string to tie the wires
- Warp and weft materials (see page 62)
- Sewing needle
- Thread to match project fabrics
- Scissors
- Rotary fabric cutter (optional)
- Cutting mat (optional)
- Medium crochet hook (F, G or H)

argyle rug

With its shifting pattern of three colors, this rug resembles intricate argyle knitting. The theory is the same as for other diamond rugs: a color repeat that is one segment shorter or longer (in this case) than the number of segments in the width of the rug. With three or more colors, the effect is even more magical than with two. It requires only careful counting as you work, and the pattern happens automatically.

I've chosen to work this rug on a standard floor loom; you can work it as well on any frame that will give you the proper width and length.

Finished Size: 22" x 45" (56cm × 114cm).

Warp:
-Red double knit cut 1¼" (3cm) wide—
    25 yards (23m).
-Yellow flocked knit cut 2" (5cm) wide—
    13 yards (12m).
-Blue jersey cut 2¼" (6cm) wide—25 yards (23m).

Wefts: Same fabric as the warps.
-Red double knit, 1¼" (3cm) wide—75 yards (69m).
-Yellow flocked knit, 2" (5cm) wide—40 yards (37m).
-Blue jersey, 2¼" (6cm) wide—75 yards (69m).

Warping Method: Warp loops.

Number of Warps: 44.

Warp Spacing: 2 per inch (25mm).

Number of Weft Rows: 90.

Weft Spacing: 2 rows per inch (25mm).

Twining Method: Countered twining.

Warping

1 | PREPARE WARP LOOPS BY COLOR

To keep the warp virtually invisible at the top and bottom edges, the warp color should match the wefts in those rows. Reading the graph from the left, the first 18 warps (9 loops) need to be red at the top and blue at the bottom. The next 9 warps are yellow at both ends, so you need 8 warps (4 loops) that are all yellow. The last yellow warp is attached to the next one that needs to be blue at the top and red at the bottom. The remaining 16 warps (8 loops) should be blue at the top, red at the bottom.

To summarize: Sew 17 loops that are half blue, half red; 4 loops all yellow; and 1 loop half yellow, ¼ red and ¼ blue. Because there was a little stretch in these fabrics (cut in the direction of least stretch), I made the loops so they would easily stretch to 45" (114cm)—about 43" (109cm) long and 86" (218cm) around—to allow for stretch during tensioning and twining.

2 | PUT WARP LOOPS ON THE WIRE

Following the top line of the graph, loop the warps on a wire, starting at the center and working outward. The yellow loops go on first. Working to the right, the 3-color loop goes next, then loops with blue at the top and red at the bottom. From the center left, there are 2 yellow loops, then 9 with red at the top and blue at the bottom.

The 3-color loop must be all yellow on the left and blue at the top of the right, so the seams will be right at the wires. Adjust all other loops so the joins are staggered but the proper color shows on the ends.

Fabric Samples
Solid colors are recommended for diamond rugs. These examples are knits that won't ravel.

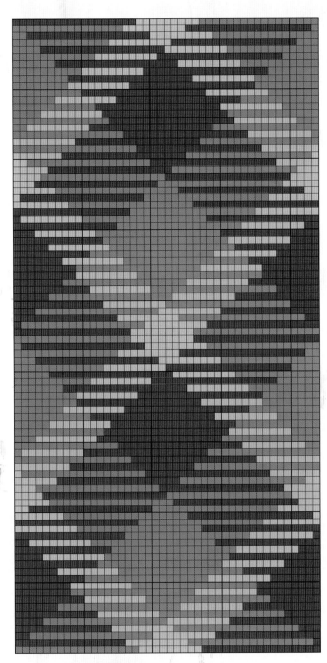

Graph for *Argyle Rug*

Follow this graph from the bottom up when working at the front of a loom, or from the top down when working at the back of a loom. The color sequence remains constant: from the top left, 18 red segments, 9 yellow, 18 blue; from the bottom left, 18 blue segments, 9 yellow, 18 red.

3| **WARPS POSITIONED ON THE BACK WIRE**
Tie the wire snugly to the back rod in several places (I used twist ties).

4| **WARPS AT THE FRONT OF THE LOOM**
Insert the 2nd wire just inside the loops in front of the 1st wire, and pull the wire to the front of the loom, keeping it on the loops. Wind the warps over the back beam and toward the warp beam (on some small looms, you will need to wind the warp around the warp beam using whatever packing method you normally use).

Extend the front rod over the breast beam toward the castle and tie the front wire closely to the rod. Tension the warps moderately but not extremely tight.

Twining

1| **MEASURE AND RECORD STRIP LENGTHS**
The 1st rows determine the length needed for each color weft. Cut 2 strips of each weft at least twice the desired width in the rug: 18" (46cm) of red, 9" (23cm) of yellow, 18" (46cm) of blue, 2 strands of each. (The blue that starts the twining can be a single strand 36" [91cm] long, folded in half to form 2 wefts). Measure and record the combined length of strips for each color (36" [91cm] red, 18" [46cm] yellow, 36" [91cm] blue).

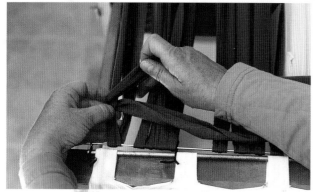

2 | START THE RUG

Because this rug requires an even number of rows, start twining at the lower left (front of the loom) with 2 blue wefts, with the ends even, not staggered. Cross wefts toward the back of the loom, with right pitch. This row is shown at the bottom of the graph.

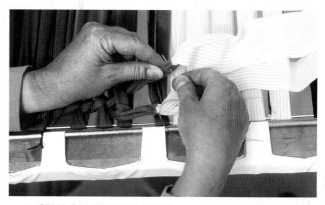

4 | SEW ON THE YELLOW

Attach yellow wefts and twine 9 segments (4½" [11cm] across).

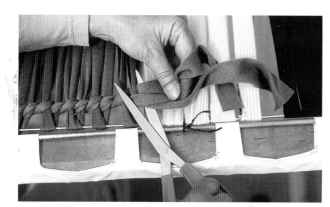

3 | CUT THE WEFTS

Twine exactly 18 segments of blue and measure to make sure this is 9" (23cm) across (2 warps per inch [25mm]). Adjust as needed.

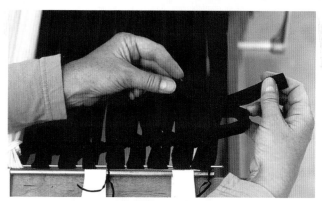

5 | TURN AT THE RIGHT SIDE

Cut both wefts, sew on red inside the yellow, and twine to the end of the row. Use the regular turn and twine 1 more segment (left pitch) to start the next row. Cut the red wefts.

Measure the leftover wefts for each color, averaging the amounts for 2 strands of each, and subtract this amount from the lengths you started with. This should give you an approximate length that you'll need for each color repeat.

Cut new wefts as before and measure after the 2nd color repeat to double-check the lengths you need. The amounts will vary a little with the weights of the fabric.

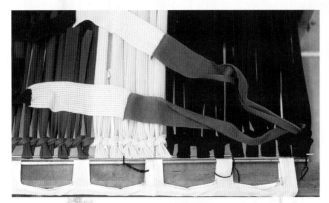

6 | START THE 2ND ROW, WITH MACHINE-JOINED WEFTS

For this rug, I needed 14" (36cm) for each red and blue weft and 7½" (19cm) of yellow. As long as you continue to count segments as you work, you should be able to machine-sew strips for 1 or 2 color repeats to speed your progress. Stitch strips straight across, with about half the seam allowance that you normally use to overlap hand-sewn strips.

Be sure to sample 1 machine-sewn length before you sew the entire weft supply, to make sure you can twine the required number of segments (and no more) with each color.

7 | START THE DIAMOND PATTERN

Continue in countered twining, always following the same color sequence, the required number of segments and a consistent warp and row spacing of 2 per inch (25mm). It will take several rows before the shifting pattern becomes apparent. Make sure the rug width remains 22" (56cm) and there are 2 weft rows per inch (25mm).

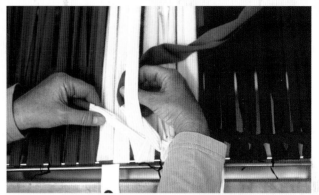

8 | START AT THE BACK OF THE LOOM

After a few rows at the front, move to the back of the loom. Start working right to left with red wefts and left pitch, then yellow, then blue, crossing wefts toward the front of the loom.

9 | WORK FROM THE FRONT AGAIN

Continue twining the predetermined distance that you measured from the back rod toward the front, winding the warp back as needed so you can reach the row you're working on. Then return to the front of the loom and complete the rug from the front.

10 | HIDE THE WEFT ENDS

Finish the rug in a solid-colored area, release the tension and remove the wires.

Taaniko Twining

Taaniko, pronounced *tah-nee-kor*, is the name for a versatile technique for which the Maori of New Zealand are famous, although the Maori do not have a rag rug tradition. The method has appeared independently in other cultures, including the Salish and Nuu-chah-nulth people of the northwest coast of North America. These people did use the taaniko technique in their twined rag rugs, producing masterpieces of complex design.

Patterns and Color

I find taaniko to be the most useful twining variation for producing complex patterns in a limited number of colors, and I use it for both rectangular and curved twining.

In a rag rug, wefts of two colors are carried throughout, but only one shows. It's possible to bring one color to the surface for a single weft segment and switch colors on the surface whenever you wish. Consequently, you can reproduce virtually any pattern you can draw on graph paper. For practical purposes, limit your designs to two or three colors per row.

Characterisitics of Taaniko

Taaniko has a similar surface texture and pitch to regular twining, although the pitch tends to be a little steeper. The back side looks quite different, without any pitch, so an item with taaniko twining is not generally reversible. Although taaniko produces a thicker textile than regular twining, both can be incorporated in the same piece, as in *A Child's Sleeping Mat* (page 68).

Two Methods

There are two ways to work taaniko. The traditional Maori way of working uses the hidden weft to wrap around the surface weft (see [A] under *Taaniko Methods* on page 67). That method tends to pull the wefts tightly until you have some experience controlling the tension. It is not as appropriate for a curved or loosely twined project as the alternate method (see [B] under *Taaniko Methods* on page 67). Experiment with both!

Patterning in Taaniko
Taaniko twining makes intricate patterning possible, such as in this rug, *Celebration*, by the author.

demonstration
taaniko methods

(A) The Maori Method

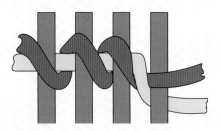

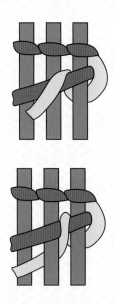

1 | WRAP THE SURFACE WEFT
Wrap the surface weft vertically with the hidden weft, then pull the hidden weft until only the surface weft shows. Keep the dominant color on the surface. Bring the hidden weft over it, top to bottom between warps, without crossing any warp. Take the hidden weft to the back side again, under the next warp, and pull it gently until it no longer shows on the surface.

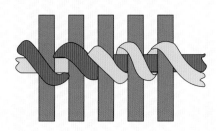

2 | CHANGE SURFACE COLORS
To change surface colors, use regular twining to exchange the weft positions, bringing the new color to the surface and the 2nd color to the back.

3 | START THE NEXT ROW WITH THE SAME SURFACE COLOR
Use the alternate turn to keep the same color on top to start the next row, if desired. Use the regular turn to change colors at the edge.

(B) Alternate Method

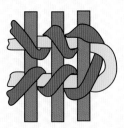

1 | WORK THE SURFACE WEFT
The alternate method (sometimes called *wrapped twining*) uses the surface weft to wrap around the hidden weft. This technique is often best for circular rugs and other projects in which you don't always want the segments as tight as possible.

Bring the surface weft (rust, above) behind, then over the other weft (blue, above), top to bottom between warps, and keep the surface weft on top of the next warp.

2 | WORK THE OTHER (HIDDEN) WEFT
Take the other weft under the warp and give it a gentle tug until it disappears. Leaving the surface weft a little looser will aid the process.

equipment and materials

- Pegged frame or loom at least
  24" × 48" (61cm × 122cm), with a
  1" (25mm) peg spacing
- Warp and weft materials
  (see page 69)
- Sewing needle
- Thread to match project fabrics
- Scissors
- Rotary fabric cutter (optional)
- Cutting mat (optional)
- Medium crochet hook (F, G or H)
- Candle or matches
  (for singeing cord)

a child's sleeping mat

Your child or grandchild will be the envy of day care with this mat for nap or play.
It features a bright border and a friendly dinosaur to inspire pleasant dream
adventures. It's especially designed to be soft, washable and lightweight enough
for a child to carry easily, yet sturdy enough for frequent use.

Finished Size: 24" × 47½" (61cm × 121cm).

Warp: White braided ³⁄₈" [10mm] nylon/polypropylene cord—65 yards (59m).

Wefts:
-Tan medium-weight polyester fleece cut ⅝" (16mm) wide—174 yards (159m).
-Green medium-weight fleece cut ⅝" (16mm) wide—64 yards (59m).

Binding: Multicolored fleece fabric cut 2½" (6cm) wide— 4½ yards (4m).

Warping Method: Continuous.

Number of Warps: 48.

Warp Spacing: Approximately 2 per inch (25mm).

Number of Weft Rows: 103.

Weft Spacing: 2 rows per inch (25mm).

Twining Method: Countered regular and taaniko twining.

Project Notes

Twining with a fleece fabric would usually produce a thick rug that might be too heavy for a small child to carry easily. I chose the equipment, fabrics, warp and twining method to make a practical mat for the purpose.

A pegged frame keeps the warp spaced for the relatively loose twining. The cord warp resists rot and mildew, so it is a good choice for a project that might need frequent washing. The fleece fabric is not only soft for comfort, it is washable.

Since fleece doesn't ravel, there is no need to turn under raw edges, which would make the mat thicker and heavier. The optional binding adds a colorful accent and helps stabilize the structure.

Preparing Warps and Wefts

1 | SINGE CUT WARP ENDS

Singe any cut ends of the cord to keep it from raveling. When sewing together warp ends and new sections of cord, overlap the pieces, pierce both thicknesses and wrap the thread around both to secure the join. The extra bulk is not a problem.

2 | PREPARING WEFTS

To reduce weft bulk, twine with the fabric flat and do not turn under the edges. This means you can cut the fabric narrower than you would for a normal rug. Normally I might use a 1" (25mm) width; half that works better for this project. However, because there's always a little compression with the twisting, I cut the fleece wefts ⅝" (16mm) wide, instead of ½" (13mm) wide.

When joining new and old wefts, overlap them and keep the fabric flat, rather than turning in the edges. Overcast the sides and tack the ends down. A slit join is an option.

Fabric Samples
The warp cord is shown at left in the photo above. Three colors of fleece form the background, dinosaur pattern and the colorful binding around the edges.

Warping

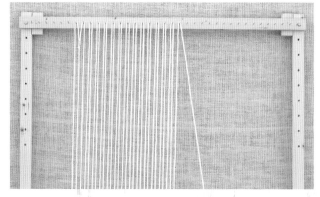

1 | PUT THE WARP ON THE FRAME

Start at the upper left of the frame and tie the cord temporarily to the 1st peg, allowing a few inches extra (note the join at upper left in the photo above).

2 | END AT UPPER RIGHT

Warp in a continuous fashion, zigzagging the cord between top and bottom pegs in order. End at the upper right (this pattern requires an even number of warps). Adjust tension and sew the warp ends to the adjacent warps.

Twining

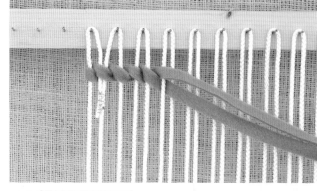

1 | START TWINING

Start with tan wefts at the upper left, using the regular turn and regular countered twining. Don't pull too tightly; maintain the spacing of 2 segments and 2 rows per inch (25mm).

2 | ROTATE THE FRAME

After a few rows at the top, rotate the frame and work from the other end with tan wefts for 6" (15cm) of weft rows.

Rotate the frame again and work most of the rest of the mat, including the patterned area, from the top side down. To center the pattern vertically, twine 11" (28cm) from the top with tan wefts in regular twining. Although the graph calls for 22 rows, mine took 24. A few extra (or fewer) is okay, but be sure it's an even number so that the 1st pattern row starts at the left.

Characteristics of Taaniko

Taaniko has a similar pitch and can be worked in countered twining, just like regular twining. However, it produces a somewhat different surface texture, and the back side is quite different. The pitch is also a little steeper, and the row spacing is a little farther apart.

The patterned area will be thicker—a bit more padding in this case. The center of the mat may be a little wider than the ends, but the ends can be stretched easily to square the mat.

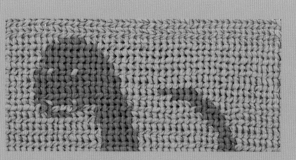

A Contrast of Textures
Note the textural difference between regular twining (the rows above the dinosaur's head) and taaniko (the patterned area).

Graph for *A Child's Sleeping Mat*

3| ATTACH A GREEN WEFT

Cut 1 of the tan wefts and attach a green weft. Use both colors for the entire patterned section, including the all-tan background areas. The center section of the mat, with the dinosaur pattern, is worked in taaniko twining (see page 67), either the wrapped twining (alternate method) or the Maori method. Measure frequently to maintain a spacing of 2 rows per inch (25mm).

Follow the graph to select which weft color to show on the surface. (For how to interpret a graph, see *Reading a Graph*, page 57.) As you work, use the previous row for reference so you don't have to count constantly.

4| FINISH THE MAT

At the end of the last pattern row, cut the green weft and attach a tan weft. Twine 2½ rows of tan with regular twining. Rotate the frame and continue with tan in regular countered twining to finish the mat.

Hand-sew the binding onto the mat, folding the binding in half lengthwise and mitering the corners.

equipment
and materials

- Pegged frame (at least 24" × 36" [61cm × 91cm], with a 1" [25mm] peg spacing) or a loom
- Warp and weft materials (see page 73)
- Sewing needle
- Thread to match project fabrics
- Scissors
- Rotary fabric cutter (optional)
- Cutting mat (optional)
- Large-eyed needle, bodkin or wire loop
- Candle or matches (for singeing cord)

toe tickler rug

You don't always have to follow the rules. This rug uses as raveled a weft as you can imagine for its special texture. The fringe makes it tricky to see the warp as you work and hides the twined structure, so it's necessary to work primarily by feel. That and the diagonal patterning are unusual, so I suggest this project for the twiner with some experience.

Finished Size: 24" × 36" (61cm × 91cm).

Warp: White braided ¼" [6mm] nylon/polypropylene cord—49 yards (45m).

Wefts:
- Tan upholstery selvedge with raveled edges, cut 1½"–2" (4cm–5cm) wide including fringe (varies)— 73 yards (67m).
- Gold upholstery selvedge with raveled edges, cut 1½"–2¼" (4cm–6cm) wide (varies)—64 yards (59m).
- Heavy green ribbed knit cut 1¾" (4cm) wide— 13 yards (12m).

Warping Method: Continuous.

Number of Warps: 48.

Warp Spacing: 2 per inch (25mm).

Number of Weft Rows: 72.

Weft Spacing: 2 rows per inch (25mm).

Twining Method: Regular countered tapestry twining and diagonal twining.

Project Notes

Industrial selvedge remnants vary in texture, fiber content and stability. The center is woven fabric that can ravel quite easily, so fold it lengthwise as you twist it into the rug. Some selvedge strips may come apart too easily to be practical, especially if they include chenille. If you can, test the fabric before you buy it to avoid strips that might be too weak. Selvedge strips can create a lot of dust, so wear a dust mask (or avoid this fabric if you have respiratory problems).

Selvedge remnants are usually sold by the pound in long sections. This rug took 1½ pounds (680g) of gold and 2¼ pounds (1,021g) of tan. I cut the green accent cloth wider than I normally would so those strips would show up better against the highly textured selvedge wefts and because the segments are larger when twined on the diagonal.

If you can't find selvedge fabric, make your own from densely woven fabrics such as denim. Cut wide strips and ravel the edges, keeping enough fabric core so the strips won't come apart completely.

Like chenille yarns, which are constructed the same way, selvedge strips look "fat" and act "skinny." A strip with long fringes and a 1"-wide (25mm) woven center will twine the same as an unfringed fabric of the same weight cut 1" (25mm) wide.

To sew wefts together by hand, overlap ends, fold lengthwise and overcast the folded edge. Don't use a slit join unless the fabric is very firmly woven.

Warping

1 | PUT THE WARP ON THE FRAME

Start at the upper left, temporarily tying the cord to the 1st peg and leaving several inches extra. Zigzag the warp between top and bottom pegs, ending at the upper right. This pattern requires an even number of warps.

Adjust tension; it should be moderately tight but not extreme.

Fabric Samples

The green fabric in the background here is used for diagonal accent stripes. On top, left to right, are the warp cord and tan and gold upholstery selvedges.

73

2 | JOIN THE END OF THE WARP TO THE 2ND WARP

Singe cut ends and stitch them to adjacent warps, sewing securely through both thicknesses of cord.

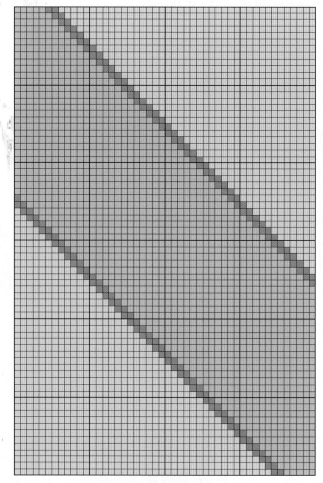

Graph for *Toe Tickler Rug*

Twining

1 | REVIEW THE DESIGN GRAPH

Following the graph on page 74, work the entire top tan section before starting the gold or green. (For how to interpret a graph, see *Reading a Graph*, page 57.) For this rug, colors decrease or increase by 1 warp on each successive row. Each row of the first tan triangle is 1 segment shorter than the previous row, starting with 41 segments and ending with 1.

This rug is worked by finishing 1 entire color section before starting the adjacent section. As long as you've counted correctly at the start and pay attention as you turn to form the diagonals, you shouldn't need to count segments as you work. Since you can't see the pitch, remember to twine (i.e., twist the wefts between the warps)!

Also, remember to maintain countered twining. It's easy to forget when you're working primarily by feel. Fortunately, the extreme texture tends to hide unintentional errors.

2 | START TWINING WITH THE TAN WEFTS

Start at the top of the frame in regular twining, left to right, on the 8th warp in from the left (counting the selvedge warp as number 1). Always use the regular turn at the selvedge, with both wefts turning around the right side warp, and continue in countered twining.

The left edge of the tan triangle forms a diagonal; maintain a spacing of 2 rows per inch (25mm) to keep this angle at 45°. Depending on your selvedge fabric, you probably don't have to compact the segments or rows as much as you normally might.

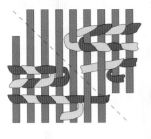

3 | TURN AT THE ANGLE, RIGHT SIDE DECREASING AND LEFT SIDE INCREASING

First turn around the weft 2 warps to the right over from the previous turn, carrying 1 weft under, then back over that warp.

4 | COMPLETE THE TURN

The 2nd weft travels 1 segment farther, under, then back over the next warp closer to the diagonal, adjacent to the warp where you just turned the other weft.

5 | START THE 1ST TURN AT THE DIAGONAL

To make a smooth angle, turn only 1 weft around each warp. On the 2nd row, 1 weft goes around the warp that is 1 to the right of the warp on which you started (thus, on the 9th warp from the left); the other weft turns around the 10th warp. Because it's hard to see which warps you used on previous rows, it helps to mark the warps you'll turn on the next time—I placed a twist tie 2 warps to the right of the previous row to mark the 1st turn on the next row.

You can turn either with the weft that goes over a warp (taking it back under the same warp going the other direction) or with the weft that naturally goes under that warp (carrying it back over the same warp). It doesn't matter, as long as you're consistent. For this rug, I chose to turn with the wefts that go under the warps. See *A Keepsake Box* (page 116) for an illustration of the other option.

6 | CONTINUE TWINING THE TAN TRIANGLE WITH A CONSISTENT ANGLE

The diagonal becomes more evident as you work. Note the marker in the photo above that shows where to turn the next weft. The last row of tan is a single segment, 20½" (52cm) down from the top. You might tape a mark to the frame temporarily at that point for reference.

Adjust rows up and down as needed (they move easily on the cord warp). Sew the weft ends together to snug the last segment, and wait until the rug is finished to hide them.

7 | TWINE THE GREEN WEFTS DOWN THE DIAGONAL

Twine a row of green wefts on the diagonal, starting on the 7th warp. Turn both around the right selvedge warp with a regular turn, and twine back up along the same diagonal, ending on the 6th warp from the left. Sew the wefts together to form the last segment, and leave the ends hanging.

8 | START THE GOLD WEFTS

On the 1st warp, start twining the gold center band with 2 gold wefts. Use the regular turn with both wefts at the left selvedge.

At the right diagonal, the wefts turn on warps number 5 and number 6. First, make the turn with the weft that goes under the 5th warp, carrying it back over that warp headed left. Next, turn the 2nd weft under, then over the 6th warp.

The next time, the wefts turn on warps number 7 and number 8. Don't turn on a warp on which you've turned before.

Twined with Upholstery Selvedges

Plush, by Dianne Rehman, was the inspiration for the *Toe Tickler* project rug.

9 | START THE DIAGONAL AT THE LEFT OF THE GOLD SECTION

The gold section leaves the selvedge on the 30th row, 14½" (37cm) down from the top. From this point until it reaches the other selvedge (just below the green rows), it will have a diagonal on each side; you must advance warp turns on the right side and decrease on the left, as the graph on page 74 illustrates. The maximum width of the gold band is 33 segments.

10 | WORK THE GOLD BAND FROM THE OTHER END, WITH THE DIAGONAL AT THE RIGHT

Rotate the frame, top to bottom, and start twining with new gold wefts on the 1st warp from the left as the frame is now positioned. The 1st row has only 5 segments, and the wefts turn on the 5th and 6th warps. Use the regular turn for both wefts around the left selvedge warp.

Mark the 33rd warp from the left side. After 1 weft turns on this warp, both leave the selvedge on the next row to form diagonals on both sides. After another row or 2, rotate the frame to its original position and complete the gold section from the top. (It's easier to see the warps when the angle is on the right side.)

Sew the final segments together and wait until later to tuck in the ends.

12 | START THE LAST TAN SECTION AT THE WIDEST POINT

Rotate the frame and start the last tan section on the 8th warp. Use the regular turn at the right selvedge and decrease each row along the left diagonal. Twine at least 6 rows.

Rotate the frame again and complete the rug from the narrow end of the tan triangle, increasing at the right side. Sew the wefts to form the last segments and remove the rug from the frame.

Use a large-eyed blunt needle to thread in all weft ends on the back side, or sew a strip temporarily to the needle to pull it through. A bodkin or fine wire loop might also work. Do not try to cut a slit in the textured wefts to pull them through with a crochet hook in the normal way, unless the fabric core is very stable.

When Warps Separate

Where the green wefts start and end at the top and bottom of the frame, the warp may tend to separate when the rug comes off the frame. I stitched through the warps at these points to help pull them together. Starting the green wefts with three rows of horizontal twining would help prevent this problem.

11 | TWINE 2 DIAGONAL ROWS WITH GREEN WEFTS

Starting at the left selvedge, twine along the diagonal with green wefts, turning at the bottom and back up to the left selvedge. Sew ends to form the last segment; leave the ends to hide later.

Chapter Five

Twining Basket-Style Rugs

Some American rug makers twined circular rugs, commonly using wheel rims to hold radiating warps under tension. Some of these were called *wagon wheel rugs*, which can include other types of rugs made on hoops. However, native people on the Pacific coast of North America twined circular and elliptical (oval) rugs as early as the late 1800s. Possibly these rugs were inspired by settlers' braided rugs, which they superficially resemble. Such rugs probably were made without any tension on the warps, derived directly from basketry traditions and constructed like the projects in this chapter.

A basket-style rug starts at or near the center; the twining spirals outward. Elliptical rugs combine features of rectangular and circular rugs, with parallel warps in the center and radiating warps at the curves. Circular rugs have radiating warps throughout.

If you're accustomed to working on a frame, the lack of warp tension takes some getting used to; but soon you'll discover the ease and versatility of manipulating the warp as well as the weft. Instead of dragging long sections of weft through a taut warp, you can cross the wefts and flip the loose warp into the twist. Also, the twist direction (pitch) stays constant. Drawbacks include the need to add warps as you work and to tuck in all the warp ends at the end.

Most curved rugs have simple concentric patterns: Adding warps could disrupt a complex pattern; a pattern worked around a curve looks more distorted than one designed on graph paper. However, the elliptical rug, a hybrid of rectangular and circular rugs, offers almost unlimited design potential if patterns are confined within the original parallel warps. Narrow pattern bands are easy to make on circular rugs, which offer opportunities to incorporate radiating patterns.

Techniques for Curved Rugs

If you are accustomed to working with warps under tension, you may find making a curved rug a little awkward at first. However, you'll quickly discover the benefits of being able to move warps rather than having to drag wefts through them. Instead, you can cross wefts, then move the warp into the twist.

Curved rugs start at the center of the warp strands and spiral outward, normally using the same pitch throughout (except, sometimes, at the start of an elliptical rug; see *Elliptical Wool Rug,* page 83). You can work clockwise (illustration A, this page) or counter-clockwise (illustration B, this page) and twist toward or away from the center. I always twist away from the center, which gives the same effect as crossing wefts on a frame toward the untwined warps.

Starting a Circular Rug

A round rug starts with evenly distributed warp strands that cross at the center. Each strand serves as two warps; the length of a warp is measured from the center of the rug. To determine the length of a strand, figure the desired diameter of the rug and add at least 4" (10cm) on each end. If, as you work, you decide to make the rug larger, you can always attach extensions to the warps. Although I usually work with full-length strands to start with, you may find it easier to start with≈shorter strands and add length to them as the rug progresses.

Start with relatively few warps to minimize the bulk at the center. Tack them together at the start or adjust them evenly after you start the rug. Sometimes a little of the warp will show at the center of a rug; if the warps and center wefts are different colors, sew on a small piece of fabric in the color you do want to show.

Because the warps are close together at the start, twine over and under two at a time for the first round only. Then twine around single warps for successive rounds.

Since the warps are not parallel, it's not necessary to use countered twining on a curved rug. It's simpler to work in a continuous spiral with a consistent pitch.

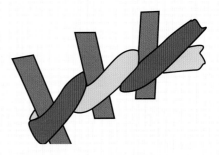

(A) Twining a Curve, Clockwise

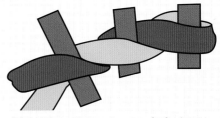

(B) Twining a Curve, Counterclockwise

Adding Warps

As the diameter of a curve increases, radiating warps (like spokes on a wheel) become farther apart, and you must twine looser as this happens in order to keep a rug flat. As weft segments become larger, you need to add warps to keep the segments small enough to be practical (about a maximum spacing of one segment per inch [25mm], with two segments per inch [25mm]a better goal). I find it easiest to add pairs of warps, temporarily attached to the previous weft row with wire twist ties. If a rug is not reversible because you're using taaniko patterning, you may prefer to loop the new warps around a weft on the underside of the previous row; the warp will show a little on that side.

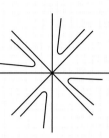

(A) Distribute New Warps Evenly

(B) Remove Ties

Adding a New Pair of Warps

Cut a new warp twice the length of the untwined existing warps; fold it at its center to serve as two new warps. Distribute new warps evenly around the curve (see [A] above), twining them in order as you come to them, pulling wefts tightly to prevent distortion. Remove ties after the following round (see [B] below). It's not always possible to distribute new warps exactly evenly; an approximation is good enough.

Distributing New Warps

To figure how many warps to add, measure the curve's circumference (the distance around the curved edge) and multiply by the desired number of warps per inch (25mm). For example, if the distance around the curve is 24" (61cm), you would need forty-eight warps for two warps per inch (25mm). If you already have thirty-six warps, you'll need to add twelve more, or six pairs. To distribute them equally, add a pair after each six existing warps. However, the circumference will increase in the next rounds before you're ready to add more warps; you may want to add even more warps at this stage, perhaps eighteen instead of twelve.

It's tedious and unnecessary to add warps on each round. In general, I add warps every three to four rounds or for each increase in radius (length from the center) of about 1½" (4cm). However, adding warps will disrupt a pattern, so sometimes I twine additional rounds to complete a pattern band first. To compensate, I may add extra warps before I start the pattern, figuring the average number needed at the middle of the pattern.

(C) Adding a Single Warp

Adding a Single Warp

Usually it's easiest to work with an even number of warps, but certain patterns require an odd number. Add a single warp by cutting a strand at least the length of the untwined portion of existing warps plus about 3" (8cm). Cut a slit near the warp's end, then use a crochet hook to pull it through several rows of weft on the reverse side, with the long end of the new warp extending between existing warps (see [C] above).

Starting an Elliptical Rug

An elliptical (oval) rug is a hybrid of a rectangular and a circular rug. The center of the rug has parallel warps, with warps radiating only on the curved sides. Warps are added only around the curves, so fewer new warps are required than for a circular rug.

As with a circular rug, each warp strand in an elliptical rug serves as two warps; warps are measured from the center. For the original warp strands, determine the desired size of the rug, top to bottom, and add at least 4" (10cm) on each end (8" [20cm] total). The number of warps depends on how wide you want this rectangular section to be and the number of desired warps per inch (25mm)—two, for example.

Lay the strands side by side, or fringe just half of a rectangle of cloth as shown in the instructions for *Elliptical Wool Rug* (page 83). Remember that some fabrics must be cut considerably wider than their eventual compressed width, so you may have to overlap individual strands of lightweight warp. Temporarily taping them to a flat surface or pinning them to a pin board might help you control them at the start.

Mark the top end of the first warp on the left with two safety pins, then the ends of the other four corner warps with single safety pins. Later, as you add warps around the curved sides, always add new warps outside these original warps.

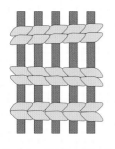

Twining Options for the Center
Top rows: same pitch, clockwise; middle rows: same pitch, counterclockwise; bottom rows: countered.

Bald Eagle
With radiating tail and wings, the bald eagle pattern adapts well to a circular rug. Some details, such as the eye and feet, were added later. *Rug by the author.*

Twining an Elliptical Rug

Twine across the centers of the parallel warps, left to right, with either left pitch or right pitch. If you wish to work the rug clockwise with right pitch (crossing wefts away from the center in the preferred manner), you may choose to work the entire center of the rug with right pitch, starting at the left. See the *Pillow* project for diagrams (Chapter Six, page 98).

Or, you can twine the center just as you would a rug, starting at the left with left pitch and using countered twining for the next row(s).

Use the regular turn at the right side and twine the second row with the same or the opposite pitch. Using countered twining for the center keeps it flatter at the start, but a same-pitch center will flatten out later when you start the spiral twining.

The shape of the center portion determines the overall shape of the rug. Multiple short rows will make a rug that's more square overall; a few long rows make a more rectangular rug. I recommend relatively few rows of back-and-forth twining at the start, to minimize distortion when you start the spiral twining.

If you wish to twine the rest of the rug counterclockwise with left pitch, end the rectangular twining at the right side. If you wish to use clockwise twining, end the rectangular twining at the left.

Patterning for Curved Rugs

While I've never seen an old round twined rug with patterning more complex than simple color bands, some interesting designs are possible. The need to add warps frequently can disrupt patterns, and I always try to add warps on solid-colored rounds where they will be less obvious.

It is possible to make some unusual designs using the taaniko technique described in Chapter Four (page 66). I usually limit these patterns to narrow bands of only a few rows, so I can twine the entire band without having to add warps.

Pattern Bands and Repeats

Pattern bands can be as simple as solid stripes or alternating colors. Successive rounds of alternating weft colors will make a radiating design if you have an even number of warps. With an odd number of warps, the same method will produce a spiraling pattern as the colors shift with each round.

When working a band with more complex taaniko patterning, pay attention to the pattern repeat and the number of warps. Like a color repeat, a pattern repeat is the fewest segments required to repeat the same pattern over and over. For example, the graph on page 82 shows a pattern repeat of six segments and will require a multiple of six warps. Before starting a repeated pattern, make sure you have enough warps so the design will come out even at the end of each round; and don't add any warps until you've finished the pattern.

Certain radiating patterns are appropriate for circular rugs, worked either in taaniko or regular twining. Consider bird designs, such as the bald eagle (see photo above) or a turkey or grouse with its tail fanned. A daisy-like flower with just a few petals works well, too.

Planning for the Appropriate Number of Warps

Detailed patterns are possible on elliptical rugs if confined to the original parallel warps. I graph my patterns first to tell me how many parallel warps I'll need. No warps are added in these sections of the rug, so pattern disruption is not a problem, and a pattern can require as many rows as needed. Other patterns that travel all the way around a rug must be confined to just a few rows and planned for the appropriate number of warps, as when twining a circular rug.

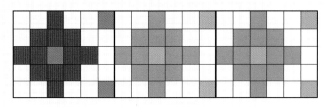

Pattern Repeat

This design has a pattern repeat of six weft segments or warps. Three repeats are shown; the darker colors are one pattern repeat.

Troubleshooting for Curved Rugs

Each successive round of a curved rug, especially a circular one, requires that you increase the size of the weft segments slightly until you are ready to add new warps. This usually happens naturally if you keep the warps at their normal spacing. If a rug starts to curl like a basket, you may be pulling wefts too tightly, stretching the warps, letting the segments become too large (because of not adding warps often enough), or working with wefts that are too narrow.

If a rug starts to ripple around the edges, it may mean you have too many warps for the circumference, or you haven't pulled the wefts tightly enough when you added new warps. It may also result from cutting strips too wide for the weight of the fabric.

Work to keep a curved rug as flat as possible, pulling wefts tightly when you add warps and letting them ease into larger segments for the next few rounds. Working flat on a table or counter can help avoid distortion and keep the rug flat.

When you add warps without wrapping the new strand around a previous weft, a small hole may be visible. Tug gently on the warps to make the spaces less obvious, or take a few stitches to pull them closed after you finish the project.

The same principles apply to other curved projects such as baskets (see chapters eight and nine, pages 112 and 125 respectively). When you want a flat base, treat it like a rug. When you want the sides to curl, deliberately pull warps and/or wefts tighter. Many first projects, intended as flat mats or rugs, end up unintentionally as baskets!

equipment and materials

- 5 safety pins
- Warp and weft materials (see page 84)
- Wire twist ties
- Sewing needle
- Thread to match project fabrics
- Scissors
- Rotary fabric cutter (optional)
- Cutting mat (optional)
- Medium crochet hook (F, G or H)

elliptical wool rug

There's something especially warm and inviting about a wool rug. In shades of orange, brown and gray, this one will warm you as you twine and warm your hearth when you're done.

Most of the patterning is simple, with a little taaniko thrown in for good measure. At two warps and rows per inch (25mm), this rug works up surprisingly quickly.

Finished Size: 22½" × 37½" (57cm × 95cm).

Warp: Brown heavy wool tweed cut ½" (13mm) wide—80 yards (73m).

Wefts:
-Orange medium-weight wool cut 1" (25mm) wide—54 yards (49m).
-Blue-gray medium-weight wool cut 1" (25mm) wide—30 yards (27m).
-Orange plaid medium-weight wool blend cut 1" (25mm) wide—25 yards (23m).
-Tan medium-weight wool blend cut 1" (25mm) wide—26 yards (24m).
-Brown heavy wool tweed (same as the warp) cut ¾" (19mm) wide—23 yards (21m).

Warping Method: Individual warps, cut in 2-warp lengths; the center warps are cut gradually from a solid rectangle of fabric.

Number of Warps: 62 at the start, 181 at the end.

Warp Spacing: Varies around the curve; 2 per inch (25mm) across the top and bottom.

Number of Weft Rows/Rounds: 4 at the center, 22 around the curve.

Weft Spacing: 2 rows/rounds per inch (25mm).

Twining Methods: Regular right-pitch and taaniko twining.

Fabric Samples
Wool and wool-blend twill fabrics in several weights comprise this rug. All-wool fabrics are recommended.

Warping

CUT THE FIRST WARPS

Cut a 15½" × 36" (39cm × 91cm) rectangle of fabric and slit it lengthwise at ½" (13mm) intervals to form the first 31 warps. Cut only halfway through the rectangle. Lay the fabric on a flat surface, warps parallel. (See *An Easier Warping Method*, page 85, for more details.)

Twining

1 | TWINE THE FIRST ROW LEFT TO RIGHT

Starting with orange wefts at the left, close to the uncut fabric, twine 4 rows back and forth using the regular turn and countered twining. (Right-pitch twining for all rows is an option; it curls the center and makes it harder to handle, but the curl disappears when you start the spiral twining).

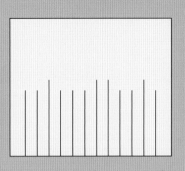

Cut the Fabric Halfway to Start the Twining

2 | CENTER THE TWINING

Slit the remainder of the fabric to separate the warps (now you have 62). Center the twining on the warps by pulling until the ends are even.

Mark the end of the first warp (top left in the photo above) with 2 safety pins, and the ends of the other corner warps (top and bottom right, bottom left) with 1 pin each. As you work the rug, keep these warps parallel and at the same spacing; add warps only on the curves outside the pins. Start all new rounds/patterns on the 1st warp.

You can start with parallel warps, cut individually and temporarily taped or pinned down to control them, or tensioned on a frame. However, Nate Jones taught me this clever warping trick that makes handling separate warp strips easier when they're not tensioned.

Cut a rectangle of fabric the length of two warps (allowing at least 4" [10cm] extra on each end) and the width needed for the desired number of warps at the appropriate width for each warp. Fringe the fabric halfway lengthwise (in the direction the warps will run), so each strip will serve as a warp but remain attached at the uncut half of the rectangle.

Twine these strips to start the rug, then cut the other half of the fabric to separate the warps. This works best if the warp width is the same as, or close to, the desired warp spacing and the warps do not need to be compressed as you twine.

3 | ADD WARPS AT THE SIDE AND START THE SPIRAL TWINING

Pins mark the ends of the parallel warps at the sides. To start the spiral twining, add 2 pairs of warps at each side. Cut four 36" (91cm) strands and fold each in half to form a pair of warps, for a total of 70 warps. Tie them temporarily to the existing warps at the sides. Future warp additions will be tied to weft rows instead of warps.

Round 1: Continue twining clockwise in spiral fashion with orange wefts, crossing them toward the outside with right pitch. The rest of the rug will be worked in same-pitch twining.

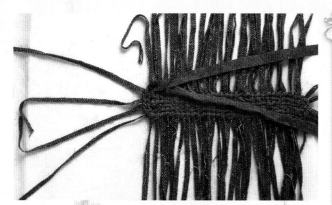

Cut as Needed

For any curved rug, cut warps as you need them, not all at once. As you work, the warps you add need only be as long as the untwined portion of existing warps, so you can cut shorter strands as the rug grows. This saves considerable fabric.

4 | START THE SECOND ROUND

ROUND 2: Starting on the 1st warp, twine with blue-gray wefts, adding 2 pairs of warps on each side, for a total of 78.

ROUND 3: Cut the weft beneath the last warp at the right and attach orange plaid. Alternate plaid and gray, starting with plaid on top of the first warp. Remove ties.

ROUND 4: Twine with 2 blue-gray wefts, adding 3 pairs of warps on each side, for a total of 90.

ROUNDS 5 AND 6: Use plaid wefts. Remove ties.

ROUND 7: Continue with plaid wefts, adding 3 pairs of warps on each side, for a total of 102.

ROUND 8: Use blue-gray wefts. Remove ties.

6 | TAKE THE TOP WEFT (BROWN) BEHIND THE OTHER WEFT

5 | ADDING A SINGLE WARP

ROUND 9: Twine with tan wefts. This is the start of the taaniko band, although the 1st and last rows use regular twining. The pattern repeat is 4 segments, so it requires a multiple of 4 warps to come out even. Add 5 pairs of warps on each side plus a single warp on each side, for a total of 124 warps.

7 | PUT THE WEFT YOU WANT TO HIDE (TAN) UNDER THE NEXT WARP

8 | GENTLY PULL THE WEFT YOU WANT TO HIDE UNTIL IT DISAPPEARS

ROUND 10: Follow the bottom 2-color line of the graphed pattern on this page using taaniko twining. Start with 2 brown segments, then 2 tan and continue all the way around. To keep a color on top, slip it behind the other weft and on top of the following warp. Slip the 2nd weft under the same warp, then pull gently until only the top color shows.

ROUND 11: Continue in taaniko with brown and tan wefts, following the middle line of the graph, starting with 1 tan segment. Repeat 2 brown, 2 tan all the way around, ending with 1 tan.

ROUND 12: Same as Round 10.

ROUND 13: Twine with 2 tan wefts, using regular twining for this row and the rest of the rug.

ROUND 14: Use orange wefts. Add 6 pairs of warps on each side (approximately after each 6 existing warps) for a total of 148 warps.

ROUND 15: Continue with orange wefts. Remove ties.

ROUND 16: To make the alternating colors that follow appear to spiral, add a single warp on 1 side, for a total of 149 warps. Twine with 1 orange weft and 1 blue-gray.

ROUNDS 17 AND 18: Continue with orange and blue-gray. Remove the tie.

ROUND 19: Twine with orange wefts.

ROUND 20: Continue with orange, adding 8 pairs of warps on each side (181 total).

ROUND 21: Twine a round with plaid wefts.

ROUND 22: Twine a row with brown wefts.

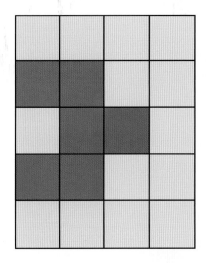

Graph for One Pattern Repeat
Read this graph from the bottom up.

Finishing the Rug

1 | HIDE THE ENDS OF THE WARPS

Sew the last segments together around the last warp on the left. Cut small slits near the weft ends.

Working on the back side of the rug, use a crochet hook to pull each weft end in alongside different warps through several rows to hide them. Do the same with each warp end, pulling it in alongside an adjacent warp on the back side. Alternate through 3 and 4 rows, working either clockwise or counterclockwise. I worked clockwise from the back, in the opposite direction from the twining.

2 | TRIM THE WARP ENDS

Make sure the warp ends don't show on the front, then trim them close to the surface.

equipment
and materials

- 1 safety pin
- Warp and weft materials
  (see page 89)
- Wire twist ties
- Sewing needle
- Thread to match project fabrics
- Scissors
- Rotary fabric cutter (optional)
- Cutting mat (optional)
- Medium crochet hook
  (F, G or H)

navajo star circular rug

The colors and patterns of Navajo rugs and baskets inspired this small rug, suitable
for your southwestern décor or any compatible design scheme. The five-pointed
star motif in the center, typical of many old Navajo wedding baskets, forms almost
magically as you twine the stair-stepped patterns around it.

Finished Size: 25½" (65cm) diameter.

Warp: Medium gray medium-weight knit cut 1¼ " (3cm) wide—54 yards (49m).

Wefts:
- Light gray checked lightweight knit cut 1¾ " (4cm) wide—60 yards (55m).
- Black ribbed lightweight knit cut 2 " (5cm) wide—37 yards (34m).
- Red velour cut 1½ " (4cm) wide—19 yards (17m).

Warping Method: Radiating warps.

Number of Warps: 8 at the start, 135 at the end.

Warp Spacing: Varies; approximately 2 per inch (25mm).

Number of Weft Rows/Rounds: 31.

Weft Spacing: 2½ rows per inch (25mm).

Twining Methods: Regular and taaniko same-pitch twining (right pitch).

Fabric Samples
Knit fabrics in gray, black and red pattern this rug. The warp fabric (lower left) is a darker shade than the gray weft. You could substitute the same fabric for warp as the weft.

Warping

CUT AND CROSS WARPS

Cut four 36" (91cm) strips and cross them at their centers, radiating outward evenly to form 8 warps. Mark 1 warp (the 1st warp) with a safety pin near its end; start new patterns on the 1st warp. Tack the strips together at the centers (optional).

Twining

1 START THE FIRST ROUND

ROUND 1: Starting clockwise around the 1st warp with gray wefts, twine over 2 warps and under 2 for the 1st round only. Cross wefts toward the outside to form right-pitch segments.

Tips on Adding Warps

When you have many warps in place and are adding a considerable number of new warps, especially if they are not distributed evenly, it helps if you first attach the twist ties all the way around. This ensures you will have the new warps where you want them.

Plan to add enough warps to complete an entire pattern band. Add warps on a solid-colored row before starting a pattern, so that the addition does not disrupt the pattern.

2 | ADD PAIRS OF WARPS

ROUNDS 2 AND 3: Continue with gray for 2 more rounds, twining over and under 1 warp at a time for the rest of the rug. At the end of the 3rd round, add 4 pairs of warps, 1 pair after each 2 existing warps, for a total of 16.

ROUNDS 4 AND 5: Continue with gray wefts. At the end of Round 5, remove the ties.

ROUND 6: Continue with gray wefts. At the end of this round, add 8 pairs of warps, 1 pair after each existing 2 warps, for a total of 32.

ROUNDS 7 AND 8: Continue with gray wefts. At the end of Round 8, remove the ties.

ROUND 9: Continue with gray wefts. At the end of this round, add 28 warps: 1 pair after the 1st and 4th existing warps; 1 pair after each of the next 6 pairs of existing warps; skip 3 and add a pair; add a pair after each of the next 4 pairs; and skip 3 and add the final pair. This will be enough warps (60) to complete the 6 pattern rows that follow.

ROUND 10: This is the final round of gray before beginning the patterning. Pull wefts tight to keep the work flat. At the end of the round, cut 1 gray weft and attach a black weft.

Step 3

Navajo Star **Chart**

Pattern bands, in sequence, starting with Round 11 (bottom) through Round 31 (top). Read these charts from bottom to top in the same order you work them. The leftmost column is the first warp.

3 | DO THE FIRST PATTERN ROW

ROUNDS 11 AND 12: In taaniko twining, twine 6 gray segments; twine (2 black, 10 gray) and repeat the sequence within parentheses 4 more times, then end with 4 gray. At the end of the 11th round, remove the ties.

ROUNDS 13 AND 14: Twine 4 gray segments; twine (6 black, 6 gray) and repeat the sequence within parentheses 4 more times, then end with 2 gray.

ROUNDS 15 AND 16: Twine (2 gray, 10 black) and repeat the sequence within parentheses 4 more times. The diameter at the end of Round 16 should be approximately 12½" (32cm). At the end of Round 16, cut both gray wefts and attach red.

4 | START THE RED BAND

ROUNDS 17 AND 18: With red wefts, use regular twining. At the end of Round 17, add 30 new warps, 1 pair after each existing 4 warps, for a total of 90. At the end of Round 18, cut both red wefts and attach 2 gray wefts.

ROUND 19: Use regular twining with gray wefts. At the end of the round, remove ties, cut 1 gray weft and attach a black weft. The diameter at this point should be approximately 14½" (37cm).

ROUND 20: In taaniko twining, twine (1 black, 5 gray) and repeat the sequence within parentheses 14 more times.

ROUND 21: In taaniko, twine (2 black, 4 gray) and repeat the sequence within parentheses 14 more times.

5 | ADD A SINGLE WARP TO MAKE THE NEXT PATTERN BAND SPIRAL

ROUND 22: In taaniko, twine (3 black, 3 gray) and repeat the sequence within parentheses 14 more times. At the end of the round, the diameter should be approximately 18" (46cm). Cut the black weft and attach gray. Add 44 warps, 1 pair after each 4 existing warps. There will be 2 extra warps at the end; add a single warp after them, just before the 1st warp. The total will be 135 warps.

ROUND 23: Use regular twining with gray wefts. At the end of the round, cut both gray wefts and attach 1 red and 1 black weft.

ROUNDS 24 THROUGH 27: Use regular twining with black and red wefts, starting with black on the 1st warp. At the end of the 24th round, remove the ties and trim the inside end of the single warp. At the end of Round 27, cut both wefts and attach gray wefts.

ROUNDS 28 THROUGH 30: Use regular twining with gray wefts. At the end of Round 30, cut gray wefts and attach black wefts.

ROUND 31: Use regular twining with black wefts. At the end of the round, sew the wefts together around the last warp to form the last segment; cut small slits near their ends and pull the ends in alongside adjacent warps for 3 or 4 rows using a crochet hook.

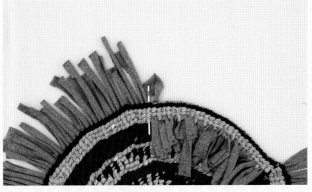

6 | HIDE THE WARP ENDS

Working on the back side, cut a small slit near the end of each warp and pull it in with a crochet hook alongside an adjacent warp, alternating through 3 and 4 weft rows. I worked counterclockwise; you may choose to work clockwise. Trim ends.

Chapter Six

Projects on Small Frames

In the past, most people who twined rag rugs used simple frames a little larger than the desired rug and made all their rugs the same length. Small frames make it easy to twine square or rectangular projects of almost any dimension. These projects are also very portable, great for taking with you as you travel. For a small investment, you can stock up on stretcher bars in a variety of sizes. Disassemble them for storage and reassemble them in different configurations to make many useful items.

Small frames are ideal for working placemats, pot holders, hot pads, mug mats, bags, purses, pillows, chair cushions and small covers for the arms and headrests of upholstered furniture. You can also make larger items by sewing small rectangular pieces together. Traditional rug twiners who wanted room-sized carpeting were known to sew smaller rugs together, removing the stitching when it was necessary to clean the components.

Consider making rag carpets for a child's dollhouse, working on a smaller scale than usual with string warps and a small frame. Be aware that any twined project designed to be thin and lightweight may take as much work and time as a rug on a larger frame! A placemat that is one-quarter the size of a rug, worked with twice the warp spacing of the rug and half the width of the same fabric weft strips, may have just as many weft segments as the larger project.

equipment
and materials

- Frame made from 20" × 16"
  (51cm × 41cm) stretcher bars,
  or similar frame with inside
  dimension of 16¾" × 12¾"
  (43cm × 32cm). Space nineteen
  1" (25mm) finishing nails across
  each end, ⅔" (17mm) apart, near
  the inside edge.
- Warp and weft materials
  (see page 94)
- Sewing needle
- Thread to match project fabrics
- Scissors
- Rotary fabric cutter (optional)
- Cutting mat (optional)
- Medium crochet hook
  (F, G or H)

placemats

Twine a set of placemats to match your tableware, using narrow strips of lightweight
fabrics, string warp and relatively loose twining to make them practical. I was lucky
to find a pair of striped cotton-blend shower curtains with the colors in my china.
This thrift-store bonanza, along with sheets from the same source, provided enough
fabric for two placemats and a table runner (page 105), or four placemats. I used
the alternate turn to make lengthwise stripes; the changing colors of the printed
fabric soften the striped effect.

Finished Size: 17¼" long × 12" wide (44cm × 30cm).

Warp: Off-white 4-ply cotton crochet yarn (about 1/16" [2mm] in diameter)—18 yards (16m) of warp per placemat.

Wefts:
-Patterned lightweight cotton or cotton-blend fabric (sheet weight) cut 1½" (4cm) wide—28 yards (26m) per placemat.
-Blue lightweight cotton or cotton-blend fabric (sheet weight) cut 1½" (4cm) wide—40 yards (37m) per placemat.
-Apricot lightweight cotton or cotton-blend fabric (sheet weight) cut 1½" (4cm) wide—7 yards (6m) per placemat.

Warping Method: Continuous.

Number of Warps: 37 (odd number recommended for lengthwise stripes).

Warp Spacing: 3 per inch (25mm).

Number of Weft Rows: 55.

Weft Spacing: 3 rows per inch (25mm).

Twining Method: Countered twining.

Fabric Samples
Choose lightweight fabrics (percale sheets or quilt fabric work well) and cut the strips narrower than you would for a rug, to reduce bulk. The apricot sheet fabric makes a good border accent.

Twining

1 | JOIN WEFTS
Join patterned and blue wefts of unequal length. Position the join at the upper left selvedge, with the patterned weft on top of the first warp.

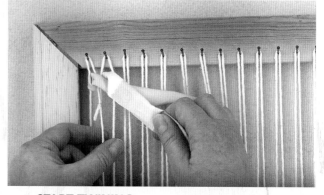

2 | START TWINING
Twine across, alternating wefts in left pitch twining and enclosing the overlapped end of the warp with the 2nd warp. Work 1–2" (25mm–51mm) down from the top of the frame. The twining should be relatively loose to keep warps aligned and spaced ⅓" (8mm) apart.

Warping

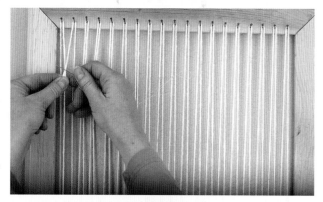

SEWING THE ENDS TO THE ADJACENT WARPS
Temporarily tie the end of the warp around the upper left nail, leaving about 3" (8cm) extra. Zigzag the warp from top to bottom, keeping it relatively taut, and end in the lower left corner. Sew warp ends to adjacent warps.

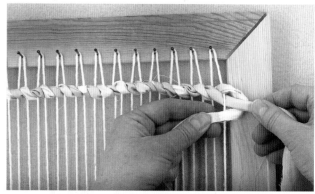

3 | START THE TURN
Use the alternate turn to keep the patterned weft on top. Bring the patterned weft behind the blue weft and keep it on top of the selvedge to start the 2nd row. Bring the blue weft under the selvedge to complete the turn.

4 | START THE 2ND ROW

5 | ADJUST THE SOLID WEFT

Place the patterned weft under the 2nd warp and resume twining. Pull the blue weft to hide it at the edge.

Twine across. Use the alternate turn at the left side to keep the patterned weft on top of the selvedge.

Push the first 2 rows up against the nails. Rotate the frame and start the other end with the patterned weft on top of the selvedge.

6 | START THE REGULAR TURN

Twine 6 rows. Use the alternate turn on each side to align the colors. Cut both wefts at the selvedge and attach apricot strips. Use the regular turn.

7 | TURN AT THE END OF THE HORIZONTAL STRIPE

Twine 3 rows with apricot wefts. Cut both at the right selvedge, attach 1 blue and 1 patterned weft, and use whichever turn will keep the patterned weft on top of the selvedge warp (shown here with the regular turn; I sewed the patterned weft on the apricot weft that was beneath the selvedge).

Rotate the frame and repeat the 3 rows of apricot wefts at the other end of the mat.

8 | WORK TOWARD THE CENTER

Continue working from both ends, rotating the frame as needed. Use the alternate turn for the rest of the center section, always keeping the patterned weft on top at the selvedges.

9 | TWINE THE LAST ROW

End anywhere in the center section, away from the sides of the frame. The last row must have the opposite pitch of the rows above and below. Finish and tuck in the wefts in the normal manner.

same-pitch twining

Same-pitch twining on curved rugs and baskets is simply a matter of working around the warps in a continuous spiral, never changing the direction of the twining. On a flat project, working rows back and forth, it's a little more challenging.

Every other row will have the *normal* pitch that you use in countered twining, crossing wefts toward the untwined warps—left pitch if you're working toward the right, right pitch if you're working toward the left (see A, this page). To keep the same pitch, work alternate rows with the pitch opposite from normal, crossing wefts *toward* the previous row of twining instead of away from it. Although this seems to come naturally to some beginning twiners, I find it more difficult than countered twining because I have to reverse directions.

Same-pitch twining with two weft colors can use either the regular or alternate turn. The regular turn (B, this page) will give the appearance of diagonal lines, like those in a twill fabric. The alternate turn (C, this page) lines up the colors vertically, creating sawtooth columns.

See the diagrams on page 97 for starting and finishing the regular turn (D1–D2 for left side, E1–E2 for right side) and the alternate turn (left and right sides, F1–F2).

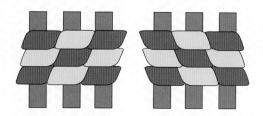

(B) Diagonals
Formed by same-pitch twining and the regular turn—right pitch (above left) and left pitch (above right).

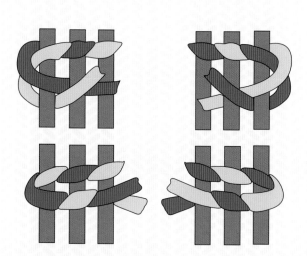

(A) Same-Pitch Twining
Right-pitch (above left) and left-pitch (above right).

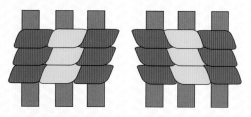

(C) Columns
Formed by same-pitch twining and the alternate turn—right pitch (above left) and left pitch (above right).

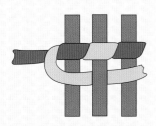

(D1) Starting the Regular Turn for Same-Pitch Twining (Left Side)

Start the regular turn with the weft under the selvedge warp, cross it over the other weft and on top of the 1st warp to start the next row. Take it under the 2nd warp and back to the surface.

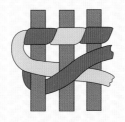

(D2) Finishing the Regular Turn for Right-Pitch Twining

The 2nd weft—the one on top of the selvedge at the end of the right-to-left row—goes under the selvedge warp to start the next row, then back to the surface.

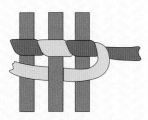

(E1) Starting the Regular Turn (Right Side)

(E2) Finishing the Regular Turn at the Right

Cross wefts bottom to top to continue twining (left pitch). The regular turn at the left side is similar.

Maintaining Proper Pitch

Just as it's easier to learn regular twining by putting one weft up over the top of the frame temporarily (page 35), you can do something similar with same-pitch twining. For example, when working right to left with left pitch, put the weft that just went under a warp down toward the bottom of the frame, then go over and under the next warp with the working weft. This will help you maintain the proper pitch.

Same-pitch twining on parallel warps introduces torque that curls the piece in diagonally opposite corners. For a bag or for the *Pillow* (page 98), this is not a serious matter, but it would be a safety concern for a rug. Restrict same-pitch twining to relatively narrow bands in a rug and be sure to use countered twining at the top and bottom to keep the corners flat.

Pillow, the next project, uses a few rows of same-pitch twining to imitate an upholstery pattern.

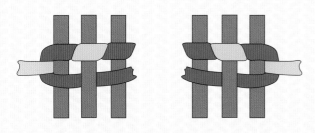

(F1) Starting the Alternate Turn (Left and Right Sides)

The alternate turn for same-pitch twining starts with the weft on top of the selvedge warp. Take it behind the other weft and keep it on top of the selvedge to start the next row. This is the same technique used for the alternate turn in countered twining, except that you immediately put that weft under the 2nd warp and back to the surface.

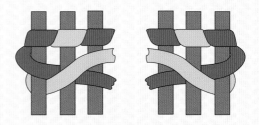

(F2) Finishing the Alternate Turn (Left and Right Sides)

Take the 2nd weft under the selvedge warp, over the 2nd warp, crossing it over the other weft toward the previous row.

equipment and materials

- Stretcher bar frame (20" [51cm] bars with inside dimensions of 16½" ×16½" [42cm × 42cm]; 17 nails 1" [25mm] apart across each end; 17½"[44cm] between nails at top and bottom
- Warp and weft materials (see page 99)
- Sewing needle
- Thread to match project fabrics
- Scissors
- Rotary fabric cutter (optional)
- Cutting mat (optional)
- Medium crochet hook (F, G or H)
- Sewing machine (recommended)
- Pillow form, 16" × 16" (41cm × 41cm)
- Hook-and-loop fastener strips, 18" (46cm)
- Coordinating fabric for pillow back, 19" x 20" (48cm × 51cm)

pillow

You can make a pillow to match your upholstery—especially if the design is a simple striped one. For more complex patterns, consider taaniko or simply using some of the upholstery fabric you're trying to match, if it's available and light-weight. Since many upholstery fabrics are too bulky or stiff for twining, you can substitute lighter-weight fabrics in appropriate colors.

This project works up quickly with its rug-weight fabrics, while the string warp makes it flexible to mold around a pillow form.

Finished Size: 16" × 17½" (41cm × 44cm), twined with the long dimension vertical but used sideways on the pillow.

Warp: Brown 4-ply cotton crochet yarn—
18 yards (16m).

Wefts:
- Tan leather-like knit cut 2" (5cm) wide—
    20 yards (18m).
- Light rust jersey cut 1¾" (4cm) wide—5 yards (5m).
- Light tan velour cut 1¾" (4cm) wide—
    14 yards (13m).
- Brown double knit cut 1¼" (3cm) wide—
    15 yards (14m).
- Orange nylon tricot, cut 3" (8cm) wide—
    6 yards (5m).
- Dark rust jersey cut 2¼" (6cm) wide—6 yards (5m).

Warping Method: Continuous.

Number of Warps: 33.

Warp Spacing: 2 per inch (25mm).

Number of Weft Rows: 43.

Weft Spacing: 2½ per inch (25mm).

Twining Methods: Countered and same-pitch twining.

Warping

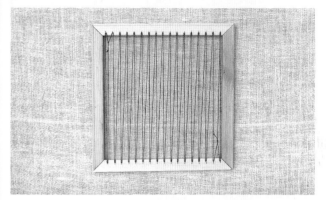

1 | START THE WARP
Start the warp at the upper left corner, leaving about 3" (8cm) extra and tying it temporarily to the upper left nail.

2 | WARP THE FRAME
Zigzag the warp from top to bottom around the nails, ending at the lower left with several inches extra. Use moderate tension. Sew the ends of the warp to the adjacent warps.

Fabric Samples
I chose these fabrics to coordinate with my upholstery—all knits that won't ravel.

Twining

1 | BEGIN TO TWINE
Start at the upper left with left pitch and tan wefts, maintaining a spacing of 2 segments per inch (25mm). Treat the warp ends as part of the warps to which they're sewn. Use the regular turn and countered twining to complete four rows.

2 | STARTING THE ALTERNATE TURN

Twine 1 row of light rust, 1 row of light tan and 1 row of brown. Cut the brown weft that's beneath the selvedge warp and sew on a light tan weft. Use the regular turn and twine a row alternating brown and light tan wefts. At the end of that row, use the alternate turn to keep light tan on top of the selvedge.

3 | SAME-PITCH TWINING, LEFT TO RIGHT

Cross wefts away from the bottom, toward the previous row, to start the next row with right pitch. The weft beneath the previous warp crosses over the other weft, bottom to top, and stays on top of the next warp.

Resume countered twining with 1 row of brown, 1 row of orange, and 10 rows of tan. Twine 1 row of light rust, 1 row of light tan, and 1 row of brown.

Sew a light tan weft to the brown weft beneath the selvedge warp, and use the regular turn to bring the light tan on top to start the next row. Twine a row alternating light tan and brown. Use the alternate turn to twine a 2nd row with light tan and brown in same-pitch (right pitch) twining.

In countered twining, work 1 row each brown, orange and light tan. In same-pitch (left pitch) twining with the alternate turn, twine 3 rows of dark rust and light tan, keeping tan on top of the selvedges.

The Other End?

Note that I didn't start twining the other end yet. Because of the asymmetrical stripes and my desire to use bands with a width similar to those in the upholstery, I waited until the pillow top was almost done (when I was able to calculate how many rows I needed of particular colors) before starting at the other end. Because this is a small project, there is little danger of crossing warps.

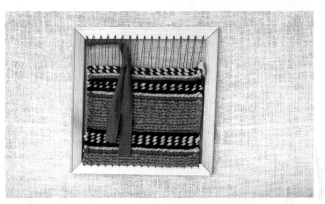

4 | STARTING THE OTHER END

Rotate the frame top to bottom and start the other end. In countered twining, complete 1 row of light rust, 3 rows of tan, 1 row of orange and 1½ rows of light tan.

5 | FINISHING THE TWINING

Rotate the frame again and work from the original direction in countered twining: 2 rows of dark rust, 1½ rows of light tan. Finish in the light tan band in the normal fashion.

Finishing the Pillow

1 | START THE PILLOW BACK

Cut a rectangle from a coordinating piece of fabric, ¾" (2cm) wider on the long sides than the pillow top and 4" (10cm) longer in the other direction. If it is a woven fabric, use the sewing machine to zigzag stitch or serge the raw edges. Press to the wrong side the ¾" (2cm) on each side and 1" (25mm) on top, adjusting as needed to make the pillow back the same size as the twined top.

2 | FINISH THE PILLOW BACK WITH POCKET

On the bottom edge, turn up 3" (8cm) to the wrong side to form a pocket, and press the fold. Sew the loop (fuzzy) side of the fastener strip just inside the fold toward the wrong side. If hand-sewing, use an overcast stitch about every ¼" (6mm) with carpet thread or doubled regular thread for strength. Sew the sides of the pocket. *Note: The photo above does not show the fastener strip, but it's easiest to add it before sewing the pocket.*

Stitch the hook side of the fastener strip just inside the bottom edge of the pillow top on the wrong side.

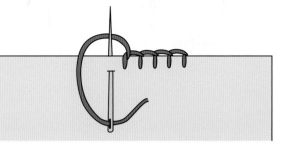

3 | SEW TOGETHER WITH THE BLANKET STITCH

With wrong sides together, hand-stitch the pillow top to the back along the sides and top, using the blanket stitch and ¼" (6mm) stitches. Use carpet thread or a doubled length of regular thread.

If you have an industrial-strength sewing machine, you may be able to machine-sew these seams very close to the edges; my machine would not handle the bulk.

4 | INSERTING THE PILLOW FORM

Slip the pillow inside the cover, tucking the bottom into the pocket on the pillow back. Close the pillow cover with the fastener strips.

Inspiration Fabric
The chair fabric inspired the pillow. The width of the finished project's striped pattern is very close to the width of the stripes on the cushion, although the scale of the weft segments is different.

Chapter Seven

Twining on a Salish Loom

A Salish-style loom, named for the Pacific Northwest people who have used this loom for more than a century, is a practical, compact frame with rollers that lets you twine a relatively long item in half the space of a conventional rectangular frame. Occasionally I've encountered similar frames with European origins, and Navajo weavers sometimes weave long rugs on their rectangular frames by folding the work around part of the frame in a similar manner.

The projects in this chapter use a small Salish loom designed for use on a table or countertop, ideal for twining a variety of useful items. See the instructions in Chapter One (page 19) for how to build a small Salish loom.

Larger Salish looms are also wonderful for rag rugs and long runners. Because your project is essentially folded in half as you work, even a rug-sized loom takes up less space than a conventional frame. Your ability to move the project around the loom as you twine helps keep the working area at a comfortable position, so you don't have to turn over a frame or work at different heights as the project progresses. Twining does proceed from both ends of the warp, however.

Salish looms also allow you to work items of various sizes on the same piece of equipment. You can change the length by moving the rollers and/or by reverse warping around spaced wires that are tied together (the space between the wires is not warped). A Salish loom made like the one used in this chapter has a base that makes it conveniently self-supporting.

Since there are no pegs on a Salish loom, you can work at any warp spacing you prefer; or simply let the fabrics and how tightly you pull the weft segments determine the ultimate spacing. This takes a bit of practice and sampling so you know how many warps are necessary to achieve a desired width.

demonstration

salish twining and reverse warping

For centuries, people of the west coast of Canada and the northwestern United States have twined mats, bags, blankets and clothing using natural materials and, more recently, rugs from strips of fabric. Their tradition of twined rag rugs dates back to about 1855; it continued into the twentieth century. Salish people of many cultures, who speak related languages, introduced a practical upright loom for weaving blankets and twining rag rugs and other items (see *Tabletop Salish Looms*, page 19).

Reverse Warping

One of the most distinctive aspects of twining on a Salish loom is the reverse warping technique that lets you create a piece with four selvedges. The warp alternates around a wire, and you can keep the area you're twining at a comfortable position by rotating the entire piece around the rollers. The warp should never travel through the inside of the frame between the rollers.

Twined Cornhusk Bag
This bag from Umatilla, Oregon, is probably of Salish origin. Narrow strips of colorful fabric form the patterning.
Collection #69155, The Field Museum.
Photo by Bobbie Irwin.

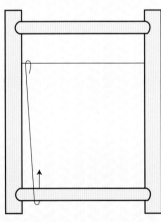

1| STARTING THE WARP
Temporarily tie the wire to the top roller a few inches down from it, then loop the start of the warp around the wire at the left side. Tie the warp temporarily to the wire.

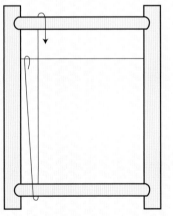

2| COMPLETING 1 ROTATION
Take the warp down around the lower roller, front to back; up the back side; over the top roller, back to front; and down the front to the wire.

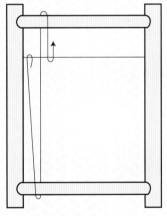

3| REVERSING THE WARPING DIRECTION
Wrap the warp around the wire (a half revolution) and reverse direction, carrying it back over the top roller.

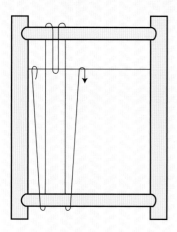

4 | WRAPPING THE WIRE FROM THE BOTTOM

Take the warp down the back side, around the bottom roller from back to front and up and around the wire, again reversing direction.

Continue until you have sufficient warps, always reversing direction when you reach the wire. The motion is a bit like that of a pendulum. Each trip around the rollers creates a single warp.

5 | FINISH THE WARPING

Ending the warp coming up from the bottom creates an even number of warps. Ending coming down from the top will make an odd number. Secure the ends of the warp to the adjacent warps that are on the same sides of the wire (above or below) and remove the ties on the wire.

Check to make sure no warps travel through the center of the frame and that you can move the entire warp and the wire all the way around the rollers.

The distance between the top of the top roller and the bottom of the lower roller is approximately half the length of the finished piece. Holes in the sides at different spacings let you adjust the distance between rollers for projects of specific lengths.

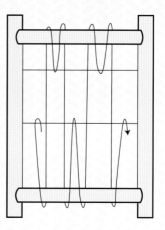

Reverse Warping Around Two Wires, for Shorter Projects

You can make shorter pieces by reverse warping around 2 wires that are tied together so that the finished length is the longer distance between the wires. Keep the wires tied together at the desired distance until the project is complete.

Reverse direction around both wires, and don't warp in the shorter space between the wires (back side of the loom).

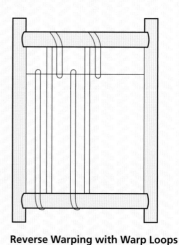

Reverse Warping with Warp Loops

It's also possible to use reverse warping with warp loops, alternating top and bottom of each loop around the wire(s).

equipment and materials

- Tabletop Salish loom with 1 wire (rollers positioned 18" [46cm] apart)
- Cardboard tube at least 2" (5cm) in diameter and at least 14" (36cm) long, slit lengthwise
- Warp and weft materials (see page 106)
- Sewing needle
- Thread to match project fabrics
- Scissors
- Rotary fabric cutter (optional)
- Cutting mat (optional)
- Medium crochet hook (F, G or H)

table runner

Twine a runner to match the placemats in Chapter Six (page 93). This project uses the same fabrics, warp and techniques. The equipment is a practical choice for making a runner twice the length of a placemat, using reverse warping around a single wire.

Since this loom has no built-in adjustment for tensioning, it's important to leave some slack in the warp to allow for the bulk of the project as it travels around the rollers. This is best accomplished by warping around one or two cardboard tube(s).

Finished Size: 37" long × 12" wide (94cm × 30cm).

Warp: Natural color 4-ply cotton crochet yarn—40 yards (37m).

Wefts:
-Patterned lightweight cotton or cotton-blend fabric (sheet weight) cut 1½" (4cm) wide—65 yards (59m).
-Blue lightweight cotton or cotton-blend fabric (sheet weight) cut 1½" (4cm) wide—70 yards (64m).
-Apricot lightweight cotton or cotton-blend fabric (sheet weight) cut 1½" (4cm) wide—7 yards (6m).

Warping Method: Continuous reverse warping.

Number of Warps: 37.

Warp Spacing: 3 per inch (25mm).

Twining Method: Countered twining, alternate turn for vertical stripes.

Fabric Samples
Choose the same fabrics used for the *Placemats* (page 93) and *Napkin Rings* (page 113), cut at similar widths.

Warping

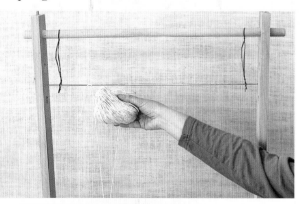

1| START THE REVERSE WARPING
Remove the top brace. Suspend the wire about 3" (8cm) down from the top roller and parallel to it. Loop 1 end of the warp around the wire at the left side, tying it temporarily with a 3" (8cm) overlap. Take the warp down around the lower roller front to back, then up the back side.

2| REVERSE DIRECTIONS AFTER WRAPPING AROUND THE WIRE
Bring the warp up over the top roller back to front, down around the wire front to back, then back over the front of the top roller.

3| CONTINUE THE WARPING
Take the warp down the back side, around the bottom roller back to front, around the wire front to back, then back down.

4| TEST FOR SLACK IN THE WARP
Leave enough slack so that you can easily fit 1 or 2 fingers between the warp and the top roller. A better option is to warp around a cardboard tube slit to fit over 1 roller or 1 tube for each roller (see *Photo Album Cover*, page 109). The tube should have a larger diameter than the roller.

5 | END OF THE WARP

Continue warping, ending at the upper right after coming down from the top roller. Count warps either above or below the wire to make sure you have 37.

6 | SEW THE END

Sew the end of the warp to the adjacent warp above the wire.

7 | SECURE THE START OF THE WARP

Sew the start of the warp to the adjacent warp below the wire. When twining, treat both ends as part of the warps to which they are attached.

8 | CHECK FOR WARP OBSTRUCTIONS

Check for crossed warps. You must be able to fit your hand between the front and back layers without obstruction. No warps should cross through the center of the frame except where they wrap around the wire. Replace the top brace.

Twining

1 | START THE FIRST ROW

Start twining below the wire on the left side, with blue weft on top of the 1st warp and patterned weft underneath. Weft lengths should be staggered.

Twine toward the right with left pitch, treating the sewn start of the warp as part of the 2nd warp. Be consistent in using the warp pairs in order, either starting with the warp on the front side or the back side of the wire. Do not twine any of the warps from the back side of the frame, however. Twine relatively loosely to maintain a 3-warp-per-inch (25mm) spacing.

Use the alternate turn at both sides to align colors vertically.

2 | START THE OTHER END

Move the 1st rows up against the wire, pulling pairs of warps to help. Temporarily remove the top brace. Keeping the wire parallel to the top roller, move the wire and twining, with the warp attached, to the back side of the frame and turn the frame around. Replace the top brace.

To start the other end, twine below the wire with 2 new wefts, working left to right, as before. If you worked the other end with the warp on the front of the wire first, use the warp on the back of the wire first for this row.

3 | TWINE THE BORDER BAND

Put the top brace in place. Continue working from either or both ends. Twine 6 rows with blue and patterned wefts, then 3 rows with apricot (on each end).

4 | WORK FROM BOTH ENDS

Twine the entire center section with blue and patterned wefts, rotating the entire warp and wire around the rollers as needed.

5 | REMOVE THE RUNNER

Finish in the center section in the interior of a row, making sure the pitch is the opposite of the rows above and below. Pull out the wire to remove the runner from the frame.

Sew wefts together to form the final segments and tuck in the weft ends to hide them.

equipment and materials

- Tabletop Salish loom with 1 wire, with dowels positioned 18"(46cm) apart
- Two 1¼" (3cm) diameter cardboard tubes at least 14" (36cm) long, slit lengthwise
- 2 long twist ties, or string
- Warp and weft materials (see page 110)
- Sewing needle
- Thread to match project fabric
- Rotary fabric cutter (optional)
- Cutting mat (optional)
- Medium crochet hook (F, G or H)
- Ring binder or photo album

photo album cover

Sometimes a colorful cloth provides all the patterning you need! Spring colors dance across this textile like flowers in an Impressionist painting. It's perfect for a June bride's album or memory book.

Narrow strips of fine fabric and a string warp minimize bulk and make this project lightweight and practical for its intended purpose. You don't have to pull wefts tightly or pack the rows firmly.

Finished Size: 12" × 37¾" (30cm × 96cm).

Warp: Bright pink 4-ply cotton crochet yarn—55 yards (50m).

Wefts: Percale sheeting (50% cotton/50% polyester) cut 1" (25mm) wide—130 yards (119m).

Warping Method: Continuous reverse warping.

Number of Warps: 48.

Number of Weft Rows: 131.

Warp Spacing: 4 rows per inch (25mm).

Twining Method: Countered twining.

Fabric Sample

This finely woven percale sheet ravels very little. A twin-sized sheet set provides plenty of fabric.

Warping

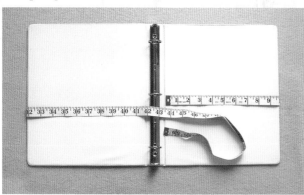

1 | MEASURE THE ALBUM OR NOTEBOOK

Measure your album or notebook starting at the inside edge of the spine. Measure around the outside of the cover and back to the spine on the other side. (Mine is 42" [107cm]). The finished project needs to cover at least half of the inside notebook covers.

Choose a dowel position on your loom that will best fit the project; I chose an 18" (46cm) distance between dowels for a cover at least 36" (91cm) in length. (Warping around cardboard tubes provides a little extra length.)

Measure the width of the notebook, top to bottom, and allow a little extra for warp width. My notebook is 11⅝" (30cm); I planned a 12"-wide (30cm) warp.

2 | BEGIN REVERSE WARPING

Place cardboard tubes, slit lengthwise, over the dowels; tie the wire temporarily to the top dowel so the wire is a few inches below and parallel to the dowel. Remove the top brace.

Loop 1 warp end around the wire, allowing at least 3" (8cm) extra, and tie it temporarily. Take the warp down around the lower dowel front to back, up the back side; around the top dowel, back to front; and around the wire front to back, headed back up.

Continue with reverse warping, always taking the warp around the outside of the dowels and reversing direction when you come to the wire. Use moderate tension.

3 | THE FINISHED WARP

For an even number of warps, end the warp around the wire coming up from the bottom. Sew warp ends to the adjacent warps below the wire. Check to make sure no warp has crossed through the center of the loom and all warps are in order at the desired spacing. The wire and the warp must be free to move all the way around the dowels without obstruction. Replace the top brace.

Twining

1 | START THE FIRST ROW

Start with 1 long weft strand folded so the ends are staggered. Starting at the left below the wire with left pitch, twine each warp in order. Treat the overlapped end as part of the 2nd warp. Be consistent about the warp order—twine the warp on the front side of the wire before the same strand on the back side of the wire. (Do not pick up any warps from the back side of the dowels, however.)

2 | TWINE THE OTHER END

Use the regular turn and countered twining. Complete 2 or 3 rows and move the wefts up to the wire. Remove the brace.

Remove ties, rotate the wire and warp to the back side, reversing the loom from back to front. Twine a row at the opposite end of the warp (now below the wire) in the same order, this time twining each warp on the back side of the wire before the same strand on the front of the wire. Put the loom brace in place and continue.

3 | APPROACHING THE FINISH

Continue working primarily from either end. Plan to finish somewhere within 5"–6" (13–15cm) of 1 end, which will be inside the notebook cover.

4 | POSITION THE ALBUM

Remove the wire and center the notebook on the textile, folding the ends evenly to the inside.

5 | STITCH THE POCKETS

By hand, stitch the side selvedges together along the doubled edges to form pockets for the notebook covers.

Chapter Eight

Three-Dimensional Twining on a Form

For many centuries, people of varied cultures have twined practical items from whatever materials they had available. Twined baskets, bags and hats are all traditional, still made by certain cultures in Africa, Asia and the Americas, usually from natural materials. Why not from fabric?

To control the shape of an object, you can use many household items as forms: pots, boxes, bowls and baskets. Use your imagination to see the potential in the objects you already have. You're not limited to what you can make on a frame!

The shape of a bowl can be duplicated in a twined textile or used to start a vessel of a more complex shape. Experiment with forms of different shapes—wide and shallow or narrow and tall—to create a variety of useful and attractive objects. Fabric twining creates a rich texture that seems warmer and more sensual than the cold, hard surface around which it was formed.

Depending on their shapes and sizes, boxes also can inspire numerous projects. In this chapter, a small box provides the shape for an elegant fabric jewelry box. A tall, narrow box, such as a cereal box, works well to shape a useful bag made all in one piece—no seams required. Even something as ordinary as a cardboard tube (see *Napkin Rings*, page 113) can inspire your fabric twining!

equipment and materials

- Cardboard tube, 1½" (4cm) diameter
- Warp and weft materials (see page 114)
- Sewing needle
- Thread to match project fabric
- Scissors
- Rotary fabric cutter (optional)
- Cutting mat (optional)
- Medium crochet hook (F, G or H)
- Tweezers (optional)

napkin rings

This project is quick and easy, yet intriguing—how do you twine a ring without a seam? It's a clever trick using a variation of warp loops, where each loop serves as one continuous warp instead of a pair.

You'll have fun making a set of these in an evening. Choose a fabric to match your placemats (page 93) and table runner (page 105). Here, I chose the apricot fabric I used for the border accent in those projects, with the warp a little closer.

Finished Size: 2" (5cm) wide, 2" (5cm) in diameter, 7½" (19cm) circumference.

Warp: 4-ply cotton crochet yarn—2 yards (2m) warp per napkin ring.

Wefts: Cotton or cotton-blend sheet fabric (percale) cut 1½" (4cm) wide—3¾ yards (3m) strips per napkin ring.

Warping Method: Continuous individual warp loops.

Number of Warps: 6.

Warp Spacing: 4 per inch (25mm).

Number of Weft Rows: 22.

Weft Spacing: 3 rows per inch (25mm).

Twining Method: Countered twining.

Warping

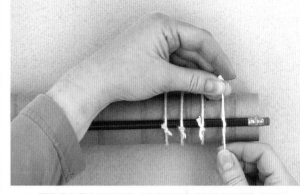

1 | TIE EACH WARP AROUND THE TUBE AND A PENCIL

Cut 8½" (21cm) lengths of yarn and tie them around the tube with square knots (see illustration below). To allow for the fabric's spacing, tie the yarn over a pencil parallel to and resting on the tube. Trim the excess and remove the pencil.

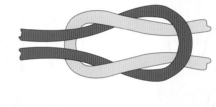

Square Knot

Fabric Sample
Any finely woven fabric, such as this percale sheet fabric, will work for weft.

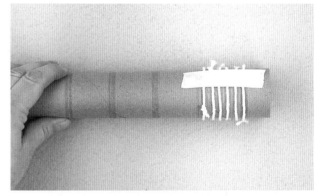

2 | POSITION WARPS ¼" (6MM) APART

Stagger the knots around the tube so no 2 are aligned. Temporarily tape down the warps, if desired, at a spacing of 4 warps per inch (25mm).

Twining

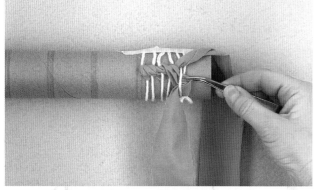

1| TWINE THE FIRST ROW
Fold 1 strip of fabric so the ends are uneven. Start twining left to right at any point, with a left pitch. You may find tweezers helpful to pull wefts through.

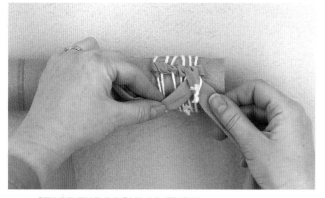

2| START THE REGULAR TURN
Use the regular turn at each side.

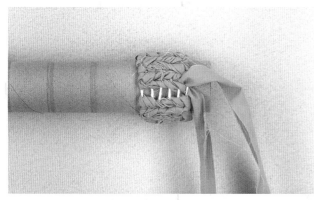

3| FINISH THE TWINING
Continue twining all the way around the tube. There's no need to work with 2 wefts from the opposite direction.

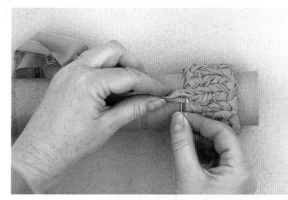

4| SEW THE LAST WEFTS TOGETHER
Finish the last row at 1 side, making sure the pitch is the opposite of the row above and below. You will have only 2 wefts at the end; sew them securely at the selvedge.

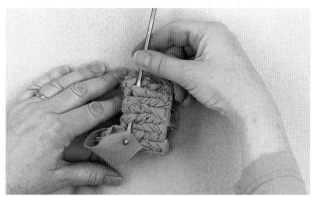

5| PULL 1 WEFT UPWARDS
Remove the ring from the tube. Pull weft ends through parallel to the 2nd warp to hide them.

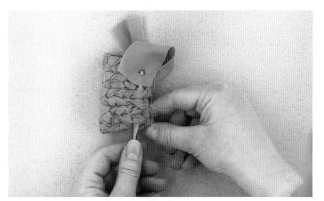

6| PULL THE OTHER WEFT DOWNWARD
Work 1 end upward and the other downward. Trim the ends to finish the ring.

equipment and materials

- Corrugated cardboard box with a hinged lid (the fabric box will end up slightly larger)
- Warp and weft materials (see page 117)
- Sewing needle
- Thread to match project fabric
- Rotary fabric cutter (optional)
- Cutting mat (optional)
- Large-eyed blunt needle (big enough for the warp), hairpin, loop of fine wire or a fine crochet hook (B, C or D)
- T-pins: 1 for every ½" (13mm) across the sides, top and front of the box
- Masking tape
- "Frog" or clasp closure
- Candle or matches (for singeing cord)

a keepsake box

An opulent fabric twined on a small cardboard box produces a tiny treasure chest for your jewelry and mementos. Use a fabric that doesn't ravel; velvet or satin ribbon would be excellent alternatives.

   This project is more challenging than it looks and is most appropriate for the twiner with some experience. The lid and base are twined separately, back and forth, and joined to the sides as part of the twining process. Sides, front and back are twined at the same time around the box.

Finished Size: 6" wide × 3½" tall × 4½" deep (15cm × 9cm × 11cm).

Warp: Black nylon-blend craft cord, $^1/_{12}$" (2mm) in diameter—15 yards (14m).

Wefts: Lightweight red velvet cut ¾" (19mm) wide—41 yards (37m).

Warping Method: Continuous for the top, back, base and front; separate continuous warps for each side.

Number of Warps: For the project box, 25 long warps, plus 14 shorter warps for each side; your number will depend on the size of the box you use.

Warp Spacing: 4 per inch (25mm).

Number of Weft Rows/Rounds: 17–19 for the top and base; 14 for the front, back and sides.

Weft Spacing: 4 rows per inch (25mm).

Twining Method: Countered twining.

Fabric Samples
A stiff nylon-blend cord (above, left) helps the box keep its shape. I used a black cord for a decorative visible accent at the top edges. Rich red velvet serves as weft.

Project Notes

Because of the way velvet both absorbs and reflects light, it is difficult to keep each segment in each row looking uniform. The changes in warp tension from start to finish can make it tricky to keep the wefts precisely at the same tension, and any variation tends to show.

With any napped fabric, and especially with velvet, it's best to cut all weft strips in the same direction and keep the same alignment throughout as you attach new wefts.

Preparing the Box

PLACE PINS FOR THE LONG WARPS

Insert T-pins firmly into the cardboard at the front top and across the front edge of the lid, starting and ending at the corners and spaced ½" (13mm) apart. Pins across the front of the lid should not be placed in the front flap. If your box length is not a multiple of ½" (13mm), add or subtract pins, then space them evenly and as close to ½" (13mm) spacing as possible. Pins should protrude at least 1" (25mm) to make warping and twining easier.

Warping

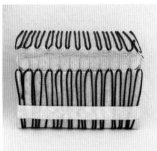

1 | PUT LONG WARPS IN PLACE

Singe the cut end of the cord. With the back of the box facing you and the lid mostly closed (flap inserted partway), loop the cord around the left corner pin in the lid, allowing a couple of inches extra, and tie it temporarily to the pin.

The warp travels toward the back of the lid, down the back of the box, across the base, up the front and around the left corner pin in front (as viewed from the back). The warp reverses direction and goes down the front, across the base, up the back and across the lid. There it wraps around the 2nd pin and reverses direction.

This motion is similar to reverse warping on a Salish loom, except the warp does not travel around a wire when it reverses direction.

2| FINISH WARPING

Continue, ending around the last pin at the top front. Cut the warp, singe the end and tie it temporarily to the last pin, allowing a couple of inches extra. Adjust the warp tension so it is even but not as tight as possible with the lid closed partway. Sew both warp ends to the adjacent warps, piercing both thicknesses of cord. Keep the pins in place for the entire project.

To prevent the warps from slipping off the edges, temporarily tape across the warp on the front and back sides. Use tape as needed to increase warp tension as you work.

The side warps are added after the lid and base are twined.

Reinforcing the Shape

Even when the warp is stiff cord, the completed box will be somewhat flexible. One option to help it hold its shape better is to work parts of the box around a fine wire armature.

For the lid, place one wire along the side (bent back on itself at the hinge), across the front of the pins and back along the other side. Wrap the warp around the wire at the front and twine it as part of the selvedge warps with the wefts.

Similarly, wrap a wire from the top back of the side, across the top of the front (enclosing it within the warp loops), then back across the other side.

Twining the Lid and Base

1| START THE LID

Start twining the lid at the front, with the front flap inserted partway, working left to right with left pitch. Use the regular turn and continue in countered twining.

Snug the wefts up tight against the pins and adjust segment tension as needed. End at the left back corner (as viewed from the back), but do not cut the wefts.

2| FINISH THE LID AND BASE

With new wefts, start the base at the front edge and work in countered twining to end at the corner directly below where the lid wefts end. **Do not** cut the wefts.

Adding the Side Warps

1| PREPARE THE SIDE PINS AND CORD

Insert the side pins into the top box edges at ½" (13mm) intervals, starting and ending ½" (13mm) from the corners. If your box side is not a multiple of ½" (13mm), space the pins evenly and use an approximate spacing of ½" (13mm).

Cut a length of cord equal to the height of the box multiplied by 2, multiplied by the number of pins in the side, plus a little extra. Singe the ends of the cord.

2 | START THE SIDE WARPS

Start warping at the upper left corner, sewing the cord end to the edge warp on the back. Go around the 1st side pin and use the needle, hairpin, wire loop or fine crochet hook to wrap the cord around the warp at the base edge (already twined). Continue zigzagging the warp around the pins and the base warp. Sew the warp end to the front selvedge warp. Repeat with a new length of cord at the other side.

Twining the Back, Sides and Front

1 | START TWINING WITH THE LID WEFTS

Twine left to right across the top of the back, maintaining the opposite pitch from the last row of the lid. Continue counterclockwise around the side, front and other side, snugging the weft up against the pins.

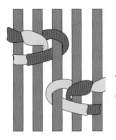

Turning Around the Corner Warp

Avoiding a Distorted Shape

The side, front and back of this box could be twined in a continuous spiral with the same pitch, but this would cause it to torque and be distorted. Same-pitch twining works for curved projects with radiating warps because the angle of the warps in relation to each other is constantly changing. However, when warps are parallel, countered twining is necessary to prevent torque. This twist might be acceptable for a bag twined on a box, but not for a finished fabric box that should maintain its shape. You have several options:
- Twine the back, sides and front as separate rectangles in countered twining, then hand-sew them together at the edges where they meet.
- Work in a continuous spiral, changing the pitch direction on one edge every time the wefts reach that point. This means that lid and base wefts must start around the sides traveling in opposite directions.
- Work around the box, turning around one edge warp and reversing direction and pitch every time you complete a round. See Step 2 (this page).

2 | BOTH LID AND BASE WEFTS TURN AROUND THE SAME CORNER WARP

After you've twined a row on all 4 sides, reverse direction by turning around the corner warp where you started (back left, as viewed from the back). Always turn on this same warp, whether working from the top or from the bottom. To reduce bulk, only the weft that normally goes over the corner warp now turns around it (over, then under as it reverses direction). The other weft turns around the previous warp (over, then under).

3 | START THE LOWER BACK

Start twining the lower back with the base wefts, with pitch opposite that of the previous base row. Twine across the back counterclockwise as you did the lid wefts. After 1 circuit, turn around the same corner warp as you did at the top and reverse direction in countered twining.

4 | TURN TO RESUME COUNTER CLOCKWISE TWINING

Continue from the top and bottom. When twining clockwise with either lid or base wefts, turn around the same corner warp in similar fashion with *only* the weft that normally would go over it; turn around the previous warp with the other weft.

End on the back side, maintaining countered twining, away from the edges. Remove pins and take the fabric off the box before hiding the wefts parallel to the warps; use a needle, hairpin, wire loop or fine crochet hook.

Center and sew on the frog or closure at the front of the box.

equipment and materials

- Pottery bowl, 4¾" (12cm) base diameter, 8" (20cm) top diameter, 4¼" (11cm) high
- Warp and weft materials (see page 121)
- Wire twist ties
- 1 safety pin, any size
- Sewing needle
- Thread to match project fabrics
- Scissors
- Rotary fabric cutter (optional)
- Cutting mat (optional)
- Medium crochet hook (F, G or H)

a basket on a bowl

When twining a basket on a bowl, it's easy to control its size and shape; the fabric warp helps hold the shape. Your twined basket will end up a little larger than the bowl you start with.

Be sure to choose a form with sides that flare outward or at least remain constant, not one that narrows above its widest point. You can twine on such a bowl, but you won't be able to get the twining off when you're done!

Finished Size: 5" (13cm) diameter base, 8" (20cm) diameter rim, 4½" (11cm) tall. Your basket will vary from this one in size and fabric requirements, depending on the size and shape bowl you use.

Warp: Turquoise cotton broadcloth cut 1½" (4cm) wide—17 yards (16m).

Wefts:
Turquoise cotton broadcloth cut 2¼" (6cm) wide—17 yards (16m).
Printed cotton broadcloth cut 2¼" (6cm) wide—10 yards (9m).

Warping Method: Radial warps.

Number of Warps: 8 to start, 53 at the end.

Warp Spacing: Varies; approximately 2 per inch (25mm).

Number of Weft Rounds: 20.

Weft Spacing: 3 rows per inch (25mm).

Twining Method: Same-pitch twining.

A Gallery of Possible Forms
The bowls on the left would work well; those on the right would work only if you stopped twining before the sides narrow.

Warping

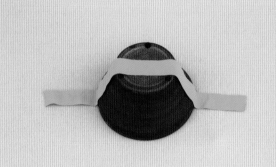

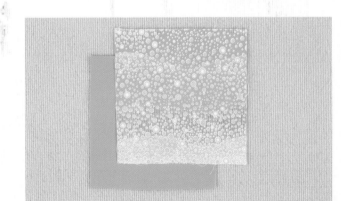

Fabric Samples
A water-splashed print fabric provides patterning in this basket. The turquoise fabric is both warp and weft.

1 | MEASURE THE WARP
Choose an appropriate bowl, place it upside down and drape a strand of warp across its widest point. Cut 4 strands, each 8" (20cm) longer than the size of the bowl. Each strand serves as 2 warps.

2 | CROSS THE WARP STRANDS
On a flat surface, cross the warp strands at their centers, radiating evenly. If you wish, tack them together at their centers to prevent shifting. Mark the end of 1 warp (the 1st warp) with a safety pin near its end. Start new patterns on this warp, and keep the pin in place until the project is finished.

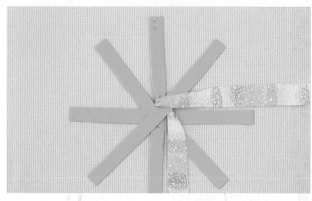

1 SPREAD THE WARPS AND START THE 1ST ROUND

ROUND 1: Fold 1 long patterned weft strip around the first 2 warps, ends offset. For the 1st round only, twine over and under 2 warps at a time. I chose to work clockwise with right pitch; you would get similar results working counterclockwise with left pitch. Cross wefts away from the center. Pull the weft segments tighter after completing the 1st round.

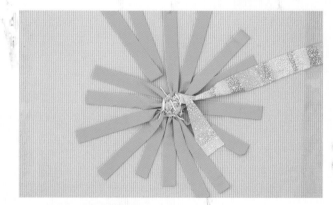

2 ADD WARPS

ROUNDS 2–3: Continue over and under 1 warp at a time for the rest of the project. At the end of the 3rd round, add 4 pairs of warps, 1 pair after each 2 original warps, for a total of 16. Adjust original warps as necessary to even the ends.

ROUNDS 4–6: Continue twining with patterned wefts. At the end of the 6th round, remove the ties.

ROUNDS 7–8: Continue twining with patterned wefts until the circle is about the same size as the base of the bowl. At the end of the 8th round, add 10 pairs of warps: 1 pair each after existing warps 1, 3, 5, 6, 7, 9, 11, 13, 14 and 16, for a total of 36 warps. Cut both patterned wefts and attach turquoise wefts.

ROUND 9: Twine with turquoise wefts for the last round of the flat base, or until slightly greater in diameter than the bottom of the bowl. Since warps and wefts are the same color, you might want to mark the ends of the wefts to distinguish them. Remember also, the wefts are a little wider.

3 BASKET BEGINS TO TAKE SHAPE

ROUND 10: Place the base on the bowl and let the warps drape over the sides. You can temporarily tape the base to the bottom of the bowl if it slides around too much. Work the rest of the basket around the upside-down bowl, conforming to its shape. Tug warps occasionally to pack the weft rounds.

Adding Enough Warps

You need enough warps at this point to complete the next round, plus the entire pattern area that follows (six rounds, or about 2" [5cm]), without adding warps that would disrupt the pattern. Calculate the number you need by multiplying by two, in inches (1" equals 25mm), the circumference of the bowl at what will be the end of the pattern area. My bowl has a circumference of 26" (66cm) at that point, requiring 52 warps at spacing of two per inch.

To make the pattern appear to spiral, I added an additional single warp, for a total of 53. It's better to have a few more warps than you need, and twine more tightly, than to have too few. I was able to complete the basket without adding warps; yours may require more.

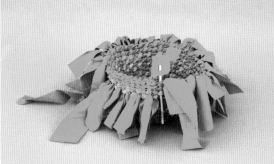

4 | ADD A SINGLE WARP

ROUND 11: Continue with turquoise wefts. At the end of this round, add 17 warps. Add 1 pair after each 4 existing warps, with a single warp instead of a pair just after the last warp, for a total of 53.

ROUND 12: This is the last round with turquoise wefts before the start of the pattern. At the end of the round, cut either weft and attach 1 patterned weft.

6 | SECURE THE WARP ENDS

ROUNDS 19–20: Finish the basket with 2 rounds of turquoise wefts. Tack weft ends together around the final warp and pull those ends into previous weft rounds alongside an adjacent warp, 1 on the inside and 1 on the outside of the basket. Similarly, pull each warp in parallel to an adjacent warp, alternating through 3 and 4 weft rounds. I worked counterclockwise on the outside, with the basket upright; you can choose to work clockwise. Trim ends.

5 | PATTERN BEGINS TO SPIRAL ON THE 2ND PATTERN ROW

ROUNDS 13–14: Continue twining with turquoise and patterned wefts. At the end of the 13th round, remove ties and trim the inside end of the single warp. As you work Round 14, the patterned fabric will be offset by 1 segment, in checkerboard fashion.

ROUNDS 15–18: Continue twining with the different wefts. At the end of Round 18, cut the patterned weft and attach a turquoise weft.

A Bit of Extra Shaping

Pulling warps in tightly caused my basket to curve in attractively at the top and made the finished diameter slightly less than that of the straight-angled pot I used as a form.

Chapter Nine

Free-Form Twining

Once you've become experienced with working curved projects without using a frame or form, you're ready to try free-form twining. A basket is an ideal starting point for this style of twining. You're not limited to a shape that expands outward, so you can create a basket that pinches in at the top or has a narrow neck.

Three-dimensional twining without a form gives you the option—and the challenge—of determining your own shapes. Basket makers have worked this way for thousands of years, although usually with stiffer natural materials. You can create one-of-a-kind accents and accessories with the freedom to change your design as you work.

While free-form twining can be liberating, it is challenging enough to recommend to the twiner with some experience. Flexible materials such as fabric seem to want to do their own thing—they may not conform to the original shape you have in mind. However, the basic techniques are the same as when working on a form or on tensioned warps. Unless your intended project has flat sides, you can use continuous same-pitch twining without the need to turn and reverse direction.

You can also start a project, such as a basket, on a form and remove it when you want to add your own embellishments of shape and ornamentation. For example, you could twine the crown of a hat on a pot, then work a brim freestyle! It's a hybrid technique that incorporates the best of both methods.

equipment and materials

- 1 safety pin (any size)
- Warp and weft materials (see page 126)
- Wire twist ties
- Sewing needle
- Thread to match project fabrics
- Scissors
- Rotary fabric cutter (optional)
- Cutting mat (optional)
- Medium crochet hook (F, G or H)

free-form basket

When you twine a basket on a form, your options for shaping are limited. Without the form, you're free to widen and narrow a basket any way you want. You can even pinch it in at the top as I did for this project basket.

A large checked fabric in multiple pastels provides color excitement for this practical and pretty basket. For a variation from some other circular projects in this book, I worked this basket counterclockwise; you'd get similar results twining clockwise.

Finished Size: 4½" (11cm) tall, 4¼" (11cm) diameter at the base, 6" (15cm) diameter at the top, 7½" (19cm) diameter at the widest point.

Warp: Rose cotton percale (from an old sheet) cut 1¾" (4cm) wide—30 yards (27m).

Weft:
– Rose cotton percale (same as the warp) cut 2¼" (6cm) wide—15 yards (14m).
– Cotton broadcloth (with 2" [5cm] pastel checks) cut 2¼" (6cm) wide—12 yards (11m).

Warping Method: Radiating.

Number of Warps: 8 to start, 48 total.

Warp Spacing: Varies; approximately 2 per inch (25mm).

Weft Spacing: 3 rows per inch (25mm).

Twining Method: Left pitch.

Fabric Samples
A solid-colored weft accents the checked fabric, which has even more colors than appear in this photo.

Warping

1| CUT WARP STRIPS
Cut 4 warp strips, each 26½" (67cm) long, to serve as 8 warps.

2| CROSS WARPS
Cross them at their centers, radiating evenly outward; tack them together if you wish. Mark the end of the 1st warp with a pin and start all pattern changes with the 1st warp.

Twining

1| START TWINING AROUND 2 WARPS AT A TIME, WORKING TOWARD THE LEFT
ROUND 1: Use the plaid fabric for both wefts to start the base. Fold a long strip around the first 2 warps so the weft ends are staggered. For the first round only, twine over 2 warps and under 2, working counterclockwise with a left pitch. Cross wefts away from the center.

2| ADD 4 PAIRS OF WARPS
ROUNDS 2-4: Continue with plaid wefts, twining this and all remaining rounds over and under 1 warp at a time. At the end of the 4th round, add 8 warps (a pair after every other original warp) for a total of 16 warps. Use twist ties around the previous weft row to secure the new warps.

3 | START TO SHAPE THE BASKET

ROUNDS 5-6: Continue with plaid wefts. At the end of the 6th round, attach 2 rose wefts and remove the twist ties. The base diameter should be approximately 4" (10cm).

ROUND 7: Start twining the sides. Pull wefts tightly and allow the warps to become more upright at an angle of about 45°. Work with the inside of the basket facing you. To distinguish same-fabric warps and wefts, remember the warps are narrower than the wefts.

At the end of the 7th round, add 16 warps, 1 pair after each 2 existing warps, for a total of 32. Keep the warps angled outward.

ROUNDS 8-10: Continue with rose wefts. At the end of the 8th round, remove the ties. At the end of the 10th round, attach 2 plaid wefts.

ROUNDS 11-12: Twine with plaid wefts. At the end of the 12th round, attach 2 rose wefts.

ROUNDS 13-15: Use rose wefts. At the start of the 14th round, attach 16 new warps, 1 pair after each 4 existing warps, for a total of 48.

5 | BASKET BECOMES NARROWER

ROUND 17: Pull the wefts tighter to curve the sides inward, angling the warps slightly toward the center.

ROUND 18: Decrease the diameter again, pulling the warps inward. This is the last of 6 rose rounds. At the end of the round attach 2 plaid wefts.

ROUNDS 19–20: Twine 2 plaid rows, steadily decreasing the diameter and circumference. As the basket narrows, check frequently for skipped or doubled warps, since the closer twining makes it harder to distinguish them. At the end of Round 20, attach 2 rose wefts. The inside diameter should be about 6" (15cm) at this point.

ROUNDS 21-22: Hold the warps horizontally toward the inside, working the last round directly inside the previous round.

Note: *If warps become too close as you are decreasing the diameter, twine 2 warps together or drop some to the inside of the basket and tuck in the ends later.*

4 | BASKET REACHES ITS MAXIMUM DIAMETER

At the end of the 15th round, remove the ties. The diameter is at its maximum, approximately 7½" (19cm).

ROUND 16: Hold the warps vertically and twine with the same circumference as the previous row.

6 | TUCK IN THE WARP ENDS

Turn the basket inside out. Sew together final weft segments; with a crochet hook, pull the ends in along adjacent warps. Tuck in each warp end along an adjacent warp, alternating through 3 and 4 rows of weft. Here, I worked in the warps clockwise; the other direction works equally well. Turn the finished basket right side out.

Chapter Ten

Twining on a Pin Board

Many years ago, weavers and bead workers discovered the versatility of working small projects on a pin board. This inexpensive and very portable piece of equipment lets you twine flat items of almost any shape, even irregular curves. You can employ the pin board over and over for different projects. Best of all, depending on the project and methods you use, all the edges of your work can be selvedges—there are no raw edges to hem and few or no warps to pull in!

The *Confetti Placemats* in this chapter offer several warping and twining options. Their shape suggests that you could twine them with radiating warps as you would a circular rug or basket: working along the curve, gradually increasing the size of the weft segments and adding warps every few rows as you work. While that approach would create smoothly angled sides, it does require tucking in the warps at the end, and the change in segment size and addition of warps might affect how it wears. One option would be to twine straight across on vertical parallel warps. This requires some tricky work with multiple short rows and turns at the upper corners, and the curves and sides will only approximate the pattern lines.

Instead of either of those methods, I chose a hybrid technique on vertical warps, following the natural curve with each row of twining. The segments are all the same size for greater stability, and the contrasting pattern bands show the curve. The drawback of this method is the stair-stepped effect on the angled sides; this does, however, have a certain attraction of its own.

equipment and materials

- Pin board to fit your pattern (mine is 31" × 18" [79cm × 46cm])
- Warp and weft materials (see page 130)
- Sewing needle
- Thread to match project fabrics
- 86 T-pins
- Tweezers (optional)
- Sturdy paper, lightweight poster board or newsprint ("roll ends" from newspaper companies)
- Felt-tipped marker
- Tracing wheel and paper (optional)
- Scissors
- Rotary fabric cutter (optional)
- Cutting mat (optional)
- Large-eyed blunt needle, wire loop or bodkin

confetti placemats for a round table

If you have a circular table, you know that rectangular placemats never really fit. Here's an attractive alternative in bright colors; twine a set and invite your friends for a summer picnic.

In contrast to the placemats in Chapter Six (page 93), I've twined these mats firmly. The string warp and close twining make them washable, a practical consideration for placemats. Consider buying a little extra plaid fabric for matching napkins!

Finished Size: 12¾" (32cm) across the top, 22" (56cm) at the base and 12" (30cm) from top to bottom.

Warp: 4-ply cotton crochet yarn—22 yards (20m) per mat. Choose a color compatible with your fabric.

Weft:
-Plaid cotton or cotton-blend fabric, or lightweight knit fabric, cut 1" (25mm) wide—68 yards (62m) per mat.
-Turquoise cotton or cotton-blend fabric, or lightweight knit fabric, cut 1" (25mm) wide—6 yards (5m) per mat.

Warping Method: Continuous.

Number of Warps: 85 (two are very short).

Warp Spacing: 4 per inch (25mm).

Number of Weft Rows: 45.

Weft Spacing: Approximately 4 rows per inch (25mm).

Twining Method: Countered twining.

Fabric Samples
This bright plaid cotton makes a lively placemat. Choose closely woven cotton or cotton-blend fabric or lightweight knit fabric. The turquoise fabric is used for the pattern bands.

I chose a coordinating multi-colored cotton crochet yarn for warp (at left) to make the mat lightweight and washable.

Prepare the Pin Board

1 | COPY AND ENLARGE THE PATTERN
Copy the pattern on this page, enlarging to 80%. The actual project pattern measures 11¼" (29cm) top to bottom and 21¼" (54cm) across at the widest point. (Because of the bulk of the fabric, the finished mat is slightly larger.)

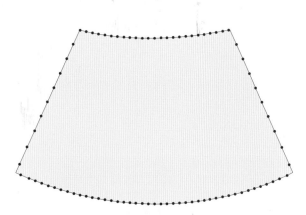

Placemat Pattern for Pin Board
Enlarge to 80%.

2 | PREPARE THE PIN BOARD
Pin the enlarged pattern to the pin board, or trace the enlarged pattern onto heavier paper or poster board.

Starting at the center, draw vertical lines with a pencil at ½" (13mm) intervals, connecting the dots. Place T-pins partway into the board where the lines intersect the pattern boundaries (at the dots on the pattern). The corners of the pattern extend slightly beyond the pin placement, and pins are farther apart on the sides than they are at the top and bottom.

The lowest pins on each side should be just slightly above the pins near the corners of the base. If your pin board is less than an inch (25mm) thick, you may need to back it with another board to keep the pins from penetrating and scratching your work surface (or you).

Warping

WARP THE PIN BOARD

Starting at the lower left corner, tie the yarn onto the lowest side pin and leave at least 4" (10cm) extra. Zigzag the warp onto the pins between bottom and side pins; the first 2 and last 2 pins are quite close together. Warp length will gradually increase.

Continue when you reach the top pins, warping the center section, then decrease warp length on the right side. End at the lower right and tie the warp around the last pin on the base, leaving at least 4" (10cm) extra. The warp should be taut, but not tight enough to move the pins.

Twining

1 | TWINING THE FIRST ROW

Note: *In the photo above, there is a knot in the warp, which was in the ball of yarn. It will be covered by the wefts.*

With plaid fabric, start twining at the upper left, following the curve, with left pitch and the regular turn. Twine firmly; snug the first row up against the top pins. Because of the firm twining and tight space around the pins (especially when starting new warps at the sides), use relatively short wefts. Due to the narrow widths, I recommend a sewn join rather than a slit join.

2 | START THE WIDER END

Rotate the board to put the wider curved edge at the top; twine along the curve with plaid fabric, starting at the left and continuing in countered twining with the regular turn. After 4 rows of plaid, attach turquoise wefts and twine 2 rows. Attach plaid wefts and continue for at least part of another row.

Rotate the board and resume at the top, adding a single row of turquoise after the first 4 rows of plaid. Rows gradually increase in length as you reach the new side warps. It's easier to twine around the new warps if you're working from the top down, so you'll probably want to work most of the mat in that direction. Twine onto the new warps at the sides at the end of a row rather than at the start.

3 | COMPLETE THE MAT

Finish the mat near the lower edge, away from the pins. Using a large-eyed needle, wire loop or bodkin, pull the wefts vertically through several weft rows to hide them. Trim the excess fabric. Use the needle to weave the warp ends up along adjacent warps for at least 2" (5cm), zigzagging them down along the next warps

Chapter Eleven

Twining on a Permanent Frame

You don't always have to remove your twining from the frame on which you worked it. Chair, stool and bench seats are excellent examples of projects for which the framework is an integral part of the completed item. Twining provides a sturdy textile that is ideal for seating. Lillie Sherwood once twined car upholstery; a correspondent told me of a man in Idaho who twined lawn chairs.

The matching seats for the project chair and stool attractively replace worn seating and give old furniture new life. For your own projects, choose furniture with open rather than solid seats—perhaps old cane, rush or fabric seats that need to be replaced. The project chair was a bargain yard sale find with an old, completely worn out leather seat. It took longer to refinish the wood than to twine the new seat!

Use a sturdy fabric that doesn't stretch in width or length. Since the warp and weft wrap around the frames and remain visible, take care to keep the "pretty side out." I chose an upholstery fabric with gold accents that coordinate nicely with the warm tones of the wood.

Chairs and stools are just some of the permanent frames you can consider. Nate Jones used fabric to twine around picture frames, mirrors and candlesticks! Some rug makers have chosen attractive frames to show off their decorative twined samplers as wall hangings. Use your imagination to envision projects twined on hoops, interesting driftwood or wire armatures—anything that you can attach a warp to. How about a twined rag flyswatter?

equipment and materials

- Stool frame
- Warp and weft materials (see page 134)
- Sewing needle
- Thread to match project fabric
- Scissors
- Rotary fabric cutter (optional)
- Cutting mat (optional)
- Medium crochet hook (F, G or H)

stool seat

Use this quick project to provide handy extra seating or for resting your feet as you relax in the matching chair (page 136). It's *not* for standing on, however!

With a project like this, there's no need to remove the warp from its frame. The process is the same for taller stools as well.

Finished Size: The stool pictured is 18" (46cm) square; the seat is 14½" × 15" (37cm × 38cm).

Warp: Heavy jacquard upholstery fabric cut 1½" (4cm) wide—12 yards (11m).

Weft: Same fabric as the warp, cut 1½" (4cm) wide—38½ yards (35m).

Warping Method: Continuous, figure-8.

Number of Warps: 23.

Warp Spacing: 2 warps = 1¼" (3cm).

Number of Weft Rows: 27.

Weft Spacing: 2 rows = 1¼" (3cm).

Twining Method: Countered twining.

Fabrics
I found that an attractive, sturdy upholstery fabric worked well for warp and weft.

Project Notes

The amount of fabric, spacing and dimensions will vary depending on the size stool you are using and the type and weight of your fabric. You may wish to make a sample on a smaller frame with suspended wires to determine your needs, or practice on the stool frame itself.

Since this heavy upholstery fabric was prone to raveling, I cut it wider than I normally would for both warp and weft (1½"[4cm] instead of an inch [25mm] wide), folded it lengthwise in thirds, then machine-stitched close to the raw edge to form a flat band. This reduced (but did not eliminate) the raveling.

Stool with Seat Material Removed
This footstool with its open wooden frame worked well for this project. The length and width of the stool are equal.

Preparation

1 | PREPARE THE CHAIR

Remove the old seat. Clean, stain and refinish the frame as needed. If the frame has one pair of dowels a little lower than the opposite pair, as does the stool in the photo above, use the lower dowels to hold the warp.

2 | PREPARE THE WARP

Prepare the warp by machine-sewing strips together, end to end, allowing a little extra length. Do not use a slit join for a weight-bearing project like this one.

Warping

1 | BEGIN WARPING

Wrap the end of the warp around the frame at the upper left, overlapping the end by at least 4" (10cm), or enough that the 1st rows of twining will cover both thicknesses. Sew the end to the same strand (the 1st fabric warp) very securely for a distance of at least 1" (25mm). Because this project remains on the frame and the wefts can't slip off, there's no need to attach the end to the 2nd warp.

2 | FIGURE-8 WARPING

Warp the frame in figure-8 fashion in a consistent direction. I took the warp over, then under 1 bar; up through the middle; over, then under the opposite bar. Because the warp remains visible where it wraps the dowels, I had to use a half twist in the center to keep the right side of the fabric showing on the dowels.

The warps cross at the center, forming a "weaver's cross" that keeps them in order and helps bring them together in a single layer.

3 | FINISH WARPING

End on either bar, depending on your sampled warp spacing and frame size. Mine, with an odd number of warps, starts and ends on diagonally opposite corners. An even number of warps works equally well; with an even number, you'd finish on the same dowel.

Pin the end temporarily and tighten the warp. You'll want firm, but not extreme, tension—tighter than you'd use for a rug or other large project. Cut and sew the end of the warp to itself as you did at the start (not to the adjacent warp), overlapping several inches and stitching securely.

Step 1: Begin Twining

Twining

1 | BEGIN TWINING

(See photo below.) With 1 long weft strand, folded with the ends staggered, start at the upper left side dowel, treating it as if it were the 1st warp. The wefts should cross between the dowel and the 1st fabric warp.

Twine straight across, left to right with left pitch, treating the overlapped end as part of the warp it's sewn to. On this stool, some of the warp at the back and front remains untwined because of the corner posts. Enclose the warps in the order in which they were put on the frame, using the cross in the center as a reference.

Treat the right side dowel as if it were the last warp, crossing wefts just before going around the dowel with both wefts, using the regular turn. Keep the right side of the fabric visible around the dowels. Cross the wefts again before starting the next row in countered twining.

Twining should be firm. Pull the wefts tightly as they turn around the side dowels. Use the regular turn around the left side dowel also, crossing wefts between the last fabric warp and the dowel. Warps remain spaced on the frame, while wefts completely cover the sides.

2 | TWINE FROM BOTH ENDS

After twining 1 or 2 rows on 1 end, rotate the stool and start the other end as you would for a rug. Pull firmly to bring the warps into the same plane. Wefts should completely cover the side dowels; warps will remain spaced on the end dowels.

3 | FINISH THE STOOL SEAT

Work from both ends. Finish anywhere away from the edges, at least 5 rows in from either end. Sew wefts together to secure the last segments; force the ends into the seat along adjacent warps, through at least 4 rows of weft. Trim the ends; cut any raveled threads.

equipment and materials

- Wooden chair with an open seat frame
- Warp and weft materials (see page 137)
- Sewing needle
- Thread to match project fabric
- Scissors
- Rotary fabric cutter (optional)
- Cutting mat (optional)
- Medium crochet hook (F, G or H)

chair seat

Give fresh life to an old chair with a new twined seat. Better yet, twine a whole set to match your décor and invite the neighbors for dinner. They'll all want to know where you found such attractive chairs—and they'll be impressed when you tell them you made the seats yourself!

Finished Size: The chair frame pictured is 18½" (47cm) across the front, 14½" (37cm) across the back and 14½" (37cm) from front to back; the seat measures 11½" (29cm) wide in back, 14½" (37cm) wide in front and 11" (28cm) deep.

Warp: Heavy jacquard upholstery fabric cut 1½" (4cm) wide—9 yards (8m) of warp.

Weft: Same fabric as the warp cut 1½" (4cm) wide—26½ yards (24m) of strips.

Warping Method: Continuous, figure-8.

Number of Warps: 22 in front, 2 outside warps on each side doubled for 18 in back.

Warp Spacing: 2 warps = 1¼" (3cm).

Number of Weft Rows: 21.

Weft Spacing: 2 rows = 1¼" (3cm).

Twining Method: Countered twining.

Project Notes

The amount of fabric, spacing and dimensions will vary depending on the size chair you are using and the type and weight of your fabric. You may wish to make a sample on a smaller frame with suspended wires to determine your needs, or practice on the chair frame itself.

Fabrics

This chair uses the same upholstery fabric as the *Stool Seat* (page 133). I prepared the fabric strips the same way; see page 134 for details.

A Good Chair for a Twining Makeover

This old chair, with its worn rawhide seat, got a complete makeover for this project: new stain, new finish and a new seat. The seat is not square—it's narrower in back.

Preparation

1 | PREPARE THE CHAIR

Remove the old chair seat. Clean and refinish the wood as needed.

2 | PREPARE THE WARP

Prepare the warp by machine-sewing strips together end to end, allowing a little extra length. Do not use a slit join for a weight-bearing project such as this one. I folded my warp and weft strips in thirds and sewed them as in the stool project (page 134) to reduce raveling.

Warping

1 | BEGIN TO WRAP THE WARPS

Wrap the end of the warp around the frame at the front left (as viewed from in front of the chair), overlapping the end by at least 4" (10cm) or enough that the 1st rows of twining will cover both thicknesses. Sew the end to the same strand (the 1st fabric warp) very securely for a distance of at least 1" (25mm). Because this project remains on the frame and the wefts can't slip off, there's no need to attach the end to the 2nd warp.

Twining

2 | START THE FIGURE-8 WARPING

Warp the frame in figure-8 fashion in a consistent direction. I took the warp over, then under the back dowel; up through the middle; over, then under the front dowel. Because the warp remains visible where it wraps the dowels, I had to use a half twist in the center to keep the right side of the fabric showing on the dowels.

The warps cross at the center, forming a "weaver's cross" that keeps them in order and helps bring them together in a single layer. The warps at the sides of the back will be spaced a little closer than those at the front, especially after you complete the 1st row of twining. Wrap enough warps for the front (wider) dowel and end at the right front.

Pin the end temporarily and tighten the warp. You'll want firm, but not extreme, tension—tighter than you'd use for a rug or other large project. Cut and sew the end of the warp to itself as you did at the start (not to the adjacent warp), overlapping several inches and stitching securely.

1 | BEGIN TWINING

Start by wrapping a long weft strand around the back left side dowel (as viewed from the front), ends staggered. Work straight across toward the right with left pitch (as viewed from the front). The wefts should cross between the dowel and the 1st fabric warp. Twine around the 1st and last 2 pairs of warps as if they were single warps, enclosing 2 pairs on each side within single weft segments. Warps 1 and 2 are twined together, as well as warps 3 and 4, 19 and 20, and 21 and 22. With the 4 doubled warps, you will have 18 segments across the back if your chair has the same measurements as this one.

Treat the right side dowel as if it were the last warp, crossing wefts just before going around the dowel with both wefts using the regular turn. Keep the right side of the fabric visible around the dowels.

Cross the wefts again before starting the next row in countered twining. Twining should be firm; pull the wefts tightly as they turn around the side dowels. Use the regular turn around the left side dowel also, crossing wefts between the last fabric warp and the dowel. Warps remain spaced on the frame, while wefts completely cover the sides.

2 | TWINE FROM BOTH ENDS

After you start the 2nd row at the back, turn the chair around so that the front dowel is away from you. Start the front end with another long weft strand, again working left to right with left pitch. Treat both overlapped ends as part of the warps to which they are sewn. Otherwise, twine each warp separately (this chair has 22 weft segments across the front).

Continue the front in countered twining for at least 5 rows (but no more than ⅓ the depth of the seat).

Rotate the chair and work the rest of the seat from the back toward the front.

3 | SPLIT THE INSIDE PAIRS OF WARPS

At approximately ⅓ of the distance from back to front, continue to twine the 1st pair of warps together, as well as the last pair of warps. However, stop doubling the inside pairs of warps and twine each separately. I did this on the 7th row from the back.

At approximately ⅔ of the way toward the front, stop doubling the remaining pairs of warps and twine each separately, as you did at the front. I did this on the 12th row from the back.

4 | FINISH THE CHAIR SEAT

Finish the seat away from the frame; stitch the last segments together securely and hide the ends by pulling them through at least 4 rows of twining, parallel to the warps.

Now sit back and relax in your newly refurbished chair, put your feet up on your new footstool and think about all the other useful and attractive items you can make with rag twining!

Lawn Chair with Twined Seat and Back
This is a practical project designed for outdoor use. The polyester cord warp and fabric resist fading and mildew better than most other fibers.

Matching Folding Stool
This is another example of how to twine on a permanent frame. I found the aluminum frame at a thrift store. Like the chair above, the stool is designed for outdoor use.

Metric Conversion Chart

To convert	to	multiply by
Inches	Centimeters	2.54
Centimeters	Inches	0.4
Feet	Centimeters	30.5
Centimeters	Feet	0.03
Yards	Meters	0.9
Meters	Yards	1.1

Fabric Yardage Needed per Yards of Strips Required

This table tells how much fabric yardage is needed if you know how many yards of strips are required. The yardages are rounded up to the nearest quarter yard.

Formula: Yardage Needed=Yards of Strips × (Strip Width ÷ Fabric Width)

Fabric Width	Strip Width	Yards of Strips Required									
		10	20	30	40	50	60	70	80	90	100
36"	1"	½	¾	1	1¼	1½	1¾	2	2¼	2¾	3
	1¼"	½	¾	1¼	1½	1¾	2¼	2½	3	3¼	3½
	1½"	½	1	1½	1¾	2¼	2¾	3	3½	4	4¼
	1¾"	½	1	1½	2	2½	3	3½	4	4½	5
	2"	¾	1¼	1¾	2¼	3	3½	4	4½	5¼	5¾
	2¼"	¾	1½	2	2¾	3¼	4	4½	5¼	5¾	6½
	2½"	¾	1½	2¼	3	3½	4¼	5	5¾	6¼	7
	2¾"	1	1¾	2½	3¼	4	4¾	5½	6¼	7	7¾
	3"	1	1¾	2½	3½	4¼	5	6	6¾	7½	8½
44"	1"	½	½	¾	1	1¼	1½	1¾	2	2¼	2½
	1¼"	½	¾	1	1¼	1½	1¾	2	2¼	2¾	3
	1½"	½	¾	1¼	1½	1¾	2¼	2½	2¾	3¼	3½
	1¾"	½	1	1¼	1¾	2	2½	3	3¼	3¾	4
	2"	½	1	1½	2	2¼	2¾	3¼	3¾	4¼	4½
	2¼"	¾	1¼	¾	2¼	2¾	3¼	3¾	4¼	4¾	5¼
	2½"	¾	1¼	1¾	2½	3	3½	4	4¾	5¼	5¾
	2¾"	¾	1½	2	2¾	3¼	4	4½	5¼	5¾	6½
	3"	¾	1½	2¼	2¾	3½	4¼	5	5½	6¼	7
65"	1"	¼	½	½	¾	¾	1	1¼	1¼	1½	1½
	1¼"	¼	½	¾	1	1	1¼	1½	1¾	1¾	2
	1½"	¼	½	¾	1	1¼	1½	1¾	2	2¼	2½
	1¾"	½	¾	1	1¼	1½	1¾	2	2¼	2½	2¾
	2"	½	¾	1	1¼	1¾	2	2¼	2½	3	3½
	2¼"	½	¾	1¼	1½	1¾	2¼	2½	3	3¼	3½
	2½"	½	1	1¼	1¾	2	2½	2¾	3¼	3½	4
	2¾"	½	1	1½	1¾	2¼	2¾	3	3½	4	4¼
	3"	½	1	1½	2	2½	3	3¼	3¾	4¼	4¾

Rag Twining References

Over the years, brief references to rag twining (especially rugs) have appeared in magazines, books and pamphlets. Most of these are out of print but available through public libraries. Very few references use the term *twining*.

Aller, Doris. *Handmade Rugs.* Lane Publishing Co., Sunset Books, 1953, pp. 76–77, 80. (One of the few references that uses the term *twined*. Illustrates checkerboard and vertical-stripe countered twining, working from the bottom up.)

Country Threads. *Rugs from Rags.* Country Threads, Inc., 1997. (Twining [here called weaving] on a pegged frame with selvedge guides, includes instructions for rug and placemat frames.)

Ferris, Grace W. "Weaving for the Cottage Porch and Summer Camp." *The Handicrafter,* June/July 1929, Vol. 1, No. 5, pp. 18–23, 37. (One of the earliest American references, this describes twining on untensioned warps hung in a door frame and illustrates tapestry and other twining pattern variations.)

Gray, Diana Blake. *Fabulous Rag Rugs from Simple Frames.* iUniverse, Lincoln, Nebraska, 2004. (Includes mention of twined rugs and instructions for others using similar equipment.)

Gustafson, Paula. *Salish Weaving.* University of Washington Press, Seattle, 1980. Also published by Douglas & McIntyre, Vancouver, 1980. (Detailed history of Salish weaving, including twining, equipment and patterning. The appendix lists Salish textiles in museum collections worldwide, including twined rag rugs.)

Irwin, Bobbie. *Twined Rag Rugs.* Krause Publications, Iola, Wisconsin, 2000. (The first full-length book ever published about twining with rags.)

Irwin, Bobbie. "Twisting Up a Rug: The Thrift and Innovation of Twined Rag Rugs," *PieceWork*, September/October 1993, pp. 64–71. (History, research and complete instructions for a small rug.)

Marr, Carolyn J. "A History of Salish Weaving: The Effects of Culture Change on a Textile Tradition," unpublished master's thesis, University of Denver, 1979. (A thorough study of Salish weaving and twining, with mention of twined rag rugs and their history.)

Ruby, Robert H. and John A. Brown, eds. *Myron Eells and the Puget Sound Indians,* Superior Publishing Co., Seattle, 1976. (Perhaps the earliest mention of twined rag rugs, described and illustrated by an amateur anthropologist and missionary in 1887.)

Tod, Osma Gallinger. "Weaving a Rug on a Frame," in *The Joy of Hand Weaving,* Van Nostrand, Princeton, N.J., 1964, Chapter 8, pp. 35–39. (Later republished by Dover. Shows *braid-weaving* on a frame from the bottom up.)

Verdier, Virginia. "Country Carpets," *Crafts 'n Things,* Summer 1981, pp. 16–18. Reprinted in May/June 1991. (Twining rag rugs on a pegged frame.)

The following references do not mention twining with rags, but they are good sources for techniques and pattern variations:

Dendel, Esther Warner. *The Basic Book of Twining.* Van Nostrand Reinhold, New York, 1978.

Harvey, Virginia I. and Harriet Tidball. *Weft Twining.* HTH Publishers, Coupeville, Washington; Shuttle Craft Guild Monograph 28, 1969.

Rag Twining Resources

Great Northern Weaving
451 E. D Ave.
Kalamazoo, MI 49007
(800) 370-7235 or (800) 446-5977
www.greatnorthernweaving.com.
(*upholstery selvedges*)

David & Gina Kuerbitz
13519 S. Hinman Rd.
Eagle, MI 48822
(517) 626-6863 or (517) 974-1662 (cell)
twinedrugsandweavings@yahoo.com
(*twining frames*)

Pattern Maker (*for cross-stitch*)
HobbyWare, Inc.
P.O. Box 501996
Indianapolis, IN 46250
(972) 562-5411
Fax: (972) 562-9287
support@hobbyware.com
www.hobbyware.com.
(*computer graphing software for easy designing*)

The Rugmaker's Homestead
www.netw.com/~rafter4/index.html
(*Rafter-four Designs offers a wealth of information online about 100+ types of rag rugs, as well as tools and supplies*)

Weavers' Cottage
(661) 269-0010 (California)
www.weaverscottage.com
info@weaverscottage.com
(*offers twining frame manufactured by Handweavers Apparatus*)

The Woolen Mill Store
8500 S.E. McLoughlin Blvd.
Portland, OR 97222
(503) 535-5786
www.pendleton-usa.com
(*Pendleton blanket selvedges*)

About the Author

A fateful chance encounter with a master rug maker in 1980 introduced Bobbie Irwin to twined rag rugs. She has been fascinated with them ever since.

Bobbie has led a worldwide revival of the disappearing craft of twining with fabric. Her first book, *Twined Rag Rugs* (Krause Publications, 2000), the first full-length book ever published about rag twining, introduced this technique to a new generation of rugmakers. Her new book, *Twist and Twine*, with even more exciting rug patterns, goes beyond rugs to explore the versatility of rag twining to create many other projects for home décor.

A weaver who lives in Montrose, Colorado, Bobbie has been a frequent contributor to textile and craft magazines. Since 1985, she has traveled throughout the United States and Canada to lecture and teach classes in rag twining, as well as numerous weaving topics. She enjoys textile research and has a special interest in reviving traditional techniques by putting them in a modern context.

Index

Explore and learn more about fiber arts!

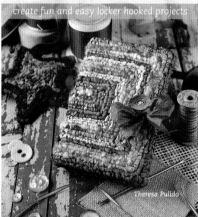

Hook, Loop & Lock
Create Fun and Easy Locker Hooked Projects

Theresa Pulido

Discover locker hooking through the colorful pages of *Hook, Loop & Lock*! Learn both traditional and innovative techniques to create a wide variety of projects such as ornaments, lamps, tote bags, rugs, game boads and much more. Theresa Pulido and her team of talented designers provide more than 25 fun and hip locker hooking projects, using a unique blend of materials such as yarn, cotton fabric strips, ribbon, silk, wool and even recycled plastic bags.

Paperback, 128 pages, #Z2273
ISBN-10: 1-60061-129-X
ISBN-13: 978-1-60061-129-2

The Woven Bag
30+ Projects from Small Looms

Noreen Crone-Findlay

With *The Woven Bag*, the size of the loom doesn't limit the size of the finished project. Clear diagrams illustrate how to assemble woven pieces into wonderful one-of-a-kind bags, pouches, totes, purses and backpacks. Author Noreen Crone-Findlay explains techniques and tricks that unlock the mysteries of weaving. Even if you've never woven before, you will soon learn how to make small looms work for you.

Paperback, 128 pages, #Z3050
ISBN-10: 0-89689-846-6
ISBN-13: 978-0-89689-846-2

Spin Dye Stitch
How to Create and Use Your Own Yarns

Jennifer Claydon

Spin Dye Stitch features everything the fiber artist needs to know to turn wool roving into beautiful one-of-a-kind handspun yarn and dyed fibers. Instead of leading the reader through boring "how-to" instructions, author Jennifer Claydon shows how to work with fibers in a practical format, with clear step-by-step photos and beautiful projects featuring knitting, weaving, embroidery and needle felting.

Paperback, 128 pages, #Z2490
ISBN-10: 1-60061-155-9
ISBN-13: 978-1-60061-155-1